Feminism in France

Feminism in France

From May '68 to Mitterrand

Claire Duchen

Routledge & Kegan Paul

London, Boston and Henley

First published in 1986
by Routledge & Kegan Paul plc

14 Leicester Square, London WC2H 7PH, England

9 Park Street, Boston, Mass. 02108, USA and

Broadway House, Newtown Road,
Henley on Thames, Oxon RG9 1EN, England

Set in 10 on 12 pt Garamond
by Inforum Ltd, Portsmouth
and printed in Great Britain
by St Edmundsbury Press,
Bury St Edmunds, Suffolk

Library of Congress Cataloging in Publication Data

Duchen, Claire.
  Feminism in France.

  1. Feminism—France—History—20th century.   2. Women
in politics—France—History—20th century.   I Title.
HQ1613.D8   1986   305.4'2'0944   85–10705

British Library CIP data also available

ISBN 0–7102–0455–8

Contents

Acknowledgements

The author and publisher would like to thank the following for permission to reproduce the illustrations in the text:

Marie-Claude Grumbach for photographs from *des femmes en mouvements* publications;

Marie Dedieu for material from *Le Torchon brûle;*

The former *Histoires d'elles* collective, through Rosi Braidotti, for material from *Histoires d'elles;*

Former *courant G* members for material from *Mignonnes, allons voir sous la rose.*

Introduction

The life of the women's liberation movement in France (the *Mouvement de Libération des Femmes*, known as the MLF) since 1968 has been exciting, volatile and puzzling to feminists from other countries. It is the evolution of the MLF, its experiences and ideas, that I want to chart in this book. In a sense, several layers are present in my approach, from simple, schematic description to a fuller, more contextualised and more clearly focused analysis which concentrates on aspects of French feminism that I think are crucial to the movement, posing as they do both exciting challenges but also very real problems. There are two main sections to the book: the first describes and analyses the productive yet conflict-ridden decade of the 1970s, looking primarily at the internal dynamic of the MLF; and the second seeks to link the MLF to its political and intellectual context in an attempt to understand its specific contours. This I do both by looking at that context, and by singling out certain important and problematic aspects of French feminism in order to explore more closely the interaction between feminism in France and the French world around it.

I have been conscious, frequently to a paralysing extent, of the dangers and difficulties involved in trying to write about the women's liberation movement, especially about the French MLF when I am not a French feminist myself. My own place within the MLF was somewhat awkward, fraught with contradictory feelings about 'studying' other feminists, committed to feminism but not committed to staying in France and knowing all the time that I was going to leave. I could not merely be an observer – nor did I want to be just an observer – but found it hard to become involved for a short time in a struggle which already had its shape defined, had its own past, and its freindship groups based on this shared experience. I never managed to resolve this in a satisfactory way, particularly as the time I spent in France (late 1980 to the beginning of 1982) was a transitional phase for the MLF, when attention was at first focused on problems that had been developing over a number of years, and later was concerned with the future of feminism in a new political environment. In spite of these difficulties, I am grateful for all the encouragement given to my project by women in France.

Most of the work for this book was done in Paris between October 1980 and the spring of 1982. During this time, the Socialists were swept to power and feminist priorities were reshuffled. Towards the end of the 1970s much energy had been spent in fighting the apparent take-over of the MLF by one group of women, who had registered the name, initials and logo of the MLF as their own commercial property – as a company title and trademark. This appropriation of the women's movement's 'official' existence was the result of a particular analysis of women's oppression and dedication to a strategy for women's liberation that was, and remains, in contradiction to an irreconcilable extent with others. This conflict is clear in the relations between this group (*Psychanalyse et Politique* – 'Psychoanalysis and Politics' – known as *Psych et Po*) and the rest of the women's movement, with the group calling itself 'anti-feminist' while co-opting the efforts of feminists and attempting to own the MLF. This tale of two, hostile women's liberation movements runs through the book. However after the election of the Left to power in 1981, the whole *Psych et Po* affair faded from centre stage. It became clear that the group was not going to enjoy the influence it had expected, and that most women were not fooled for long about what the MLF had now become: the ownership of the name became more of a nuisance than a real threat. It was the relation of the women's movement to the Socialist Government and to political institutions in general that came to the fore. This has raised questions for the MLF of strategy and power, alliances and co-option, autonomy and dependence especially concerning the issue of the Ministry for Women's Rights set up by the government in 1981. This is another of the main threads of the MLF story in this book.

Every woman has her own experience of feminism and of the

women's liberation movement, identifies herself as she chooses and as she can. The MLF that is presented here will be recognisable to some women and possibly not to others. Its most obvious limitation is that it is Paris-centred. This was for practical reasons: in Paris there was the greatest availability of documents, the presence of many groups and events, and last – but not at all least – because I had almost free accommodation for nearly a year and a half. If I had gone to Marseilles, to a steel town in Lorraine or to a village in Brittany, I would probably have formed different impressions. Each situation or experience has its measure of general validity and its own particularity. I hope to have shown some of the range of approach and experience within the MLF while acknowledging its Parisian bias, and do not claim to provide an exhaustive picture of the French women's movement. I would add, though, that as far as France is concerned, the situation of the women's movement is similar to that of other social and political movements: the spearhead is in the capital and, with certain regional differences, other areas of France may follow with a time lapse. The women's movement tends to be strong in urban areas and in university towns, while it may remain unknown in the more rural areas where traditional family structures and attitudes still dominate.

The book follows my own interests and preoccupations which are also the questions that I believe are crucial for the MLF. On the one hand, discussion of the 'concept of the feminine' pursues my own incomplete – and now abandoned – seduction by the idea; and the second focus, that of life on the political margins examined through the case of feminism in the French Socialist Party and through looking at feminism in political institutions in general, is pertinent to all feminists who live and work with institutions of one kind or another. For me, it is a daily confrontation with the constraints and limitations of an educational institution, but the experiences of women in political parties mirror those of women in all institutions.

*　　　*　　　*

Thanks are due to many people, as always, for support of many kinds. Some will be surprised to see their names but I am grateful to them all: Jocelyne Bagnès, Betsy Brewer, Susan Cohen, the Explorations in Feminism collective, Jill Lewis, Sian Reynolds, Ailbhe Smyth, Kate Turley, Ben Mandelson and my mother, Myra Duchen.

In October 1984 I went to Paris to 'interview' a number of women involved in various ways in feminism in France and I would like to thank them for participating in this work and for their hospitality: Françoise Ducrocq, Liliane Kandel, Nadja Ringart; Oristelle Bonis, Marie-Jo Dhavernas, Françoise Duroux, Françoise Gollain, Hélène Rouch; Odette Brun, C. Andrée Cabada, Josée Cantegreil, Anne le Gall, Françoise Grux, Edith Lhuillier, Solange Maurice, Marie-Claude Ripert, Lucette Soskis; Noelle Moreau, Colette Guillaumin, Claudie Lesselier, Nicole-Claude Mathieu; Rosi Braidotti; Danielle Haase-Dubosc. Special thanks to Rosi, Danielle, Claudie, Josée and Françoise Ducrocq for organising the groups with whom I talked. Most of the discussions, which concentrated on the whole on recent developments in the MLF, are to be found in Chapter 7, but parts of them have found their way into different sections of the book, to re-tell a story, to add a comment on, or a new perspective to, the topic under discussion.

A word on style. I have called feminists 'they' throughout, which no doubt reflects my own ambivalence about where I was speaking from in relation to the French women's movement. I felt uncomfortable with both 'we' and 'they': I could not honestly say 'we' as most of what I discuss took place in my absence. Saying 'we' would have felt as though I was pretending that I had been there all the time. On the other hand, 'they' sounds as though I divorce myself from feminism which is of course not so. I settled on 'they' because it felt less dishonest. I am not a French feminist and it is really their story, which as an almost outsider (but not quite), as a sister sharing some of it (but not all), I have tried to tell.

When I refer to the MLF, unless it is stated otherwise, I am referring to all those individuals and groups of women who consider themselves to be part of the women's liberation movement. The MLF as the name of the Association founded by the group *Psychanalyse et Politique* is called *Psych et Po* or *MLF marque déposée* throughout, to make the distinction between this group and feminism clear.

A word on translation: all quotations from the French are my own translations except where credit is given to another translator. Sometimes when more than one meaning is possible (or intentional) as is frequently the case, I have put in several choices. When the nuances contained in the French are impossible to translate and need explanation, I have added a footnote.

It remains only to be said that all interpretations and errors in the text are my sole responsibility.

Claire Duchen

CHAPTER 1

Beginnings

Feminism in France was not invented in May '68; there was by then already a long tradition of women fighting for a better life for women. These women, mostly isolated and ignored, often imprisoned and sometimes killed, struggled for women's civil and political rights in the context of the society they lived in, or sought to change that society through a socialist revolution, and linked their struggle to the struggle of the working class. Largely forgotten by history, it was only after the emergence of the 'new' feminism, significantly different in many ways from the 'old', that women began to look back, uncover and reclaim as their heritage the words and actions of their foremothers.

During the French Revolution of 1789, women demonstrated for price ceilings on bread and flour as they had always done when their families' subsistence level was threatened, but they also demanded political rights for the first time, wanted the right to participate in public life on the same footing as men. Like men, they formed political clubs of their own (as they were not permitted to join most of the men's clubs), wrote in newspapers, demanding education for girls and reform of the marriage laws, and showed concern for the 'public good' and public morality rather than for themselves. One woman's voice stood out: Olympe de Gouges rewrote the *Declaration of the Rights of Man* in 1791, substituting Woman for Man wherever it occurred and was ridiculed for her efforts. (She was guillotined, however, because she supported the king, not for her feminism.) Revolutionary men proved to be as misogynistic as any others, and women's activity was suppressed by revolutionaries and reactionaries alike.

By the mid-nineteenth century, women's political activity largely fitted into a schema of 'reform versus revolution' which set different perspectives in opposition to each other. On the one hand, women became involved in Utopian or revolutionary socialist movements, inspired by Henri de Saint-Simon, Charles Fourier or Louis Blanc, while on the other, they pressed for reforms through legislation concerning women's status in French society. Women did not see themselves as sharing a common 'condition', a common lot, but created their identity along class lines. There were moments when these class lines were crossed, such as in 1832 when women joined together to produce a women's political newspaper and proclaimed that 'Women, up till now, have been exploited, tyrannised. This tyranny, this exploitation must stop. We are born free, like men, and half the human race cannot justifiably be enslaved to the other.'[1] These women defined themselves as Utopian socialists and working class, and broke the tradition whereby working-class women demonstrated for economic reasons while middle-class women wrote and talked with ideological motivations. The 1832 experiment was repeated during the 1848 revolution, when a daily feminist newspaper was founded by women, bourgeoise Eugénie Niboyet and proletarians Jeanne Deroin and Suzanne Voilquin, who wanted the new French Republic to be truly republican and apply 'Liberty, fraternity, equality' to women as to men. Probably the best known feminist of this time is Flora Tristan, who has retrospectively been acclaimed as the first socialist feminist, believing that the struggle of workers and of women for their emancipation could not be successful without the support of the other, as it was ultimately the same struggle. It was Tristan who said, before Engels, that 'The most oppressed man can oppress someone else – his wife. She is the proletarian's proletarian.'[2] Tristan lived as an outsider and a nomad, dying at the age of 39. Her words were not heard during her lifetime, and the euphoric moments of women working together, regardless of social origin and status, were even more shortlived than the revolutions that inspired them.

By the time of the Third Republic (1871), differences between women of different social class were exaggerated rather than minimised. Socialist men denied that the reforms demanded by feminist associations could benefit working-class women, and insisted that 'feminist' meant 'bourgeois' and that therefore feminists

2

were enemies of socialism. One woman bridged the widening gap between reform and revolution, speaking out as a socialist for women's political rights. Hubertine Auclert led the small suffragist movement and opposed the distinction between middle-class and working-class women saying '. . . The only difference between most rich and poor women is the status of the man whose mission it is to exploit them'. The dominant attitude, however, was expressed by German socialist Clara Zetkin, in a statement made by the first International Congress of Socialist Women in 1907, saying flatly that on no account should socialist women ally themselves with bourgeois feminists. The tension between the socialist movement in France and feminism has never been resolved.[3]

What came to be identified as 'feminism' by the eve of the First World War was primarily philanthropic and reformist, with over 123 feminist organisations working to make Republican society more comfortable for women of all classes. There were 35 feminist newspapers produced between 1875 and 1914, representing the entire spectrum of women's interests from newspapers advocating education for girls to literary reviews. The most prestigious and ambitious of these was *La Fronde* a newspaper founded in 1897 by ex-actress Marguerite Durand and run entirely by women. Well-respected, the paper stressed pacifism, laicism, education as well as discussing the situation of women at work and advocating women's political rights. *La Fronde* expressed its opinions about all the issues of the day, and managed to do what no other feminist paper has tried to do since: keep going as a women's, feminist, daily paper for six years.

The two heated issues of early twentieth century feminism in France were the constant question of women's allegiance to class or to sex and the question of women's suffrage. Suffragism had never been a determined, violent campaign in France mainly because of the influence that the Catholic church had over women. The male politicians most likely to sponsor women's right to vote – left-wing Republicans and socialists – hesitated because they felt that a vote by a woman was a vote for the church, which was obviously against the programme of the Left. Women were given the vote only in 1944 by General de Gaulle, and even then everyone had reservations about it: on the Right, it was believed that the vote, together with increasing numbers of women in the workforce, would mean the death of traditional values, the end of the family and a drop in the birth rate; the Left was still afraid that women's vote would be reactionary; and most women felt that it wouldn't change a thing.

In fact it did change things: once women were citizens, part of the electorate, politicians had to woo them. Everyone was fighting for the 'female vote' which they believed existed, in spite of lack of evidence. It also clearly altered women's relation to political parties, in which they were allowed to participate, as members and as candidates, for the first time. A new set of problems emerged, concerning the disparity between political rights on paper and women's experiences inside political parties, which contributed to the total disaffection for party procedures of many politically active women, and still causes problems for those feminists who try to remain active inside political parties today.

Women continued to fight for change outside parliament, in 'reformist' associations. One campaign in particular was fought outside parliament long before it became a central political issue: the campaign for the legalisation of contraception, and later, the legalisation of abortion. The *Mouvement Français pour le Planning Familial* (the French Family Planning Association) paved the way for the eventual reform of the repressive 1920 law prohibiting abortion and of the outlawing of information about, and provision of, contraception. This matter was brought into political circulation by the 1965 presidential campaign of François Mitterrand who favoured the legalisation of contraception. The 1967 *loi Neuwirth* made this a reality, allowing feminists in the 1970s to concentrate on the abortion issue.

Women in the 1950s and 1960s participated in political parties and in pressure groups as well as continuing traditionally 'women's' activity in voluntary associations, charities and social work. Even one of the most outspoken women active in the 1950s, Simone de Beauvoir, did not see an agenda for the emancipation of women outside the agenda of the Left. By the mid-1960s, then, there were already different types of women's political involvement, different types of feminism and strong influences on the women who were later to be part of the *Mouvement de Libération des Femmes*. There are profound differences between the MLF and previous feminisms, but there are also many continuities, similar experiences, problems and issues shared by 'new' and 'old' feminism.

Nor was the 'new' feminism, the MLF, born in isolation from other political thinking in the late 1960s. Many of the ideas and practices that appeared in the MLF were shared by others: marginal political parties; extra-parliamentary 'revolutionary' groups; specific interest groups such as the ecologists and the homosexual FHAR. Those who formed this culture of protest were all opposed to the authoritarian, centralised state of Gaullist France, were all dismissive of parliamentary politics and trade union organisation, but, apart from their agreement over what they rejected, had no agreement about what they wanted. Probably the most powerful expression of this alternative revolt, which has had a lasting effect on political expression in France, was during the events of May 1968.

May '68 was an expression of anger, disillusionment, rejection. Although the outbreak of violence was unforeseen, it is retrospectively possible to see it as the culmination of a revolt directed against the stifling educational system and, by extension, against the social system of which the university is a part. In 1967, a number of students in Strasbourg, together with members of the Situationist International,[4] produced a pamphlet criticising university education and student life. Daniel Cohn-Bendit, who became one of the principal spokesmen of the May Movement, took up some of the most important aspects of the Strasbourg critique, and described the university system as a 'sausage machine, which turns people out without any real culture and incapable of thinking for themselves, but trained to fit into the economic system of a highly industrialised society'.[5] The protestors of May '68 believed that the university was part of a system that demanded passive support but no participation, encouraged isolation rather than community, required exploitation to maintain itself, and routine to keep people regimented and defeated.

The student and other protestors who formed the May Movement came from extreme Left groups, with all shades of anarchists, Marxists, Trotskyists, Maoists, socialists and others represented. They refused to oppose the government in traditional ways, believing that to follow established channels of opposition was merely to become implicated in the system they were rejecting. 'Politics' was perceived as sterile and incapable of changing society; the May Movement wanted to act differently, be different, and show that something else was possible. Rejecting organisation and strategy, the strength and specific character of the May Movement lay in its spontaneity, its lack of hierarchy and its disorder. Disorder and lack of specific goal was hailed as something positive. Participants claimed that it allowed people to step out of their usual routine, to talk to each other in ways that hadn't happened before, changing the atmosphere in Paris and showing how the stifling daily routine summed up by *métro-boulot-dodo* (metro-work-sleep) repressed the individual's potential for a creative, fulfilling life.

The importance of May '68 was not ultimately in its results for the political system, but in its reality as experience for those who were involved, in the effects it had on individual lives. The term *soixante-huitard* was coined to describe those whose optimism, energy and utopian vision now seems unrealistic, nostalgic and naive in the post-recession, nuclear-anxious 1980s, but which seemed to open up new potential for political intervention, and for living lives differently in 1968. Those who participated felt that the events of May '68 challenged and destabilised a regime that had seemed unshakable. Daniel Cohn-Bendit said to Jean-Paul Sartre in an interview that they had 'exploded the major obstacle – the myth that no-one could do anything to shake the regime. We've proved that this isn't true.'[6] May '68 showed that politics was not a matter of parliamentary games and electoral battles, but was about how people lived and what they did, how they interacted. Barriers were broken, both the content and the modes of political action were affected, and in this moment of rupture with the political boundaries of the Fifth Republic, May '68 profoundly influenced the style and content of the women's movement which emerged in its wake. The influence was both positive and negative: on the one hand, there was the unquestionable political influence on the MLF, the circulation of new, exciting ideas; on the other, there was the negative way in which women activists experienced their role and status in the events – and it was ultimately the negative side of women's experience during the events that led to the formation of an autonomous movement for women's liberation.

One of the most vociferous and influential groups in the May Movement was the *Mouvement du 22 mars* (the 22 March Movement, so named because 6 of its members were arrested on this date), a loosely organised group which included anarchists, and communists among others. They believed in the personal responsibility of each individual for her or his political journey, withdrew unconditional faith in leaders and rejected the division between those who know and tell and those who are told and obey. Rather than talking about the oppression of others (the Third World, the working class), they believed in fighting for their own liberation in the light of their own oppression. Rather than set up a 'correct political line' and act accordingly, they believed in a permanent readjustment of theory and practice in the light of personal experience, and in constant self-criticism.

These attitudes constituted an absolute break with established practices whether Revolutionary or not, and helped to develop new ideas about revolutionary practice with which the protestors of the May Movement could identify. The anti-authority and anti-hierarchy basis of these new political ideas greatly influenced the way that the MLF was to operate. The way that women experienced the events, however, took them away from the mixed organisations with which they had been involved, and led to the formulation of the concept of sexual politics, which, as an examination of sexual and social relations deriving from a gendered social hierarchy, did not yet exist.

French women activists' experience during the May events was similar to that of American women involved in civil rights movements and student politics and to that of British women in the New Left. Women's political ideas and actions often hinged on what their husbands or their boyfriends were doing and thinking: association with important men was generally women's access route to prominence. Yet once they were involved in politics, the sexual division of labour left something to be desired and the euphoria of the moment was tempered by the anger they felt at the way male militants treated them. Women were generally the ones who saw that chores were done and people were fed rather than being at the heart of the discussion and the decision-making. Women felt that they were ignored or put down by the men, and that the tasks they were given, or expected to carry out, were menial and mechanical. One woman later wrote of her feelings angrily: 'when they are involved in "serious men's talk", we really have to battle to have a turn to speak, and then when we've finished, we might as well not have bothered, they haven't even been listening . . .'[7]

Almost inevitably, women responded to this humiliation and frustration with silence. A woman signing her name as J.K. wrote in the first collection of feminist papers published in 1970,[8] pointing out how women seemed to have the choice either to play at being secretaries, or to become more like men in their approach, because the ability to think and speak seemed to be the exclusive privilege of the men. Even worse was the way that many women simply accepted this role. J.K. continues talking about her own experience by saying that: 'I decided to simply do my best, telling myself that although I wasn't capable of thinking or speaking, at least I would be the one who made the best photocopies.' Gradually, however, women became angry at the disparity between male revolutionary speech and their behaviour where women were concerned. Men didn't seem to realise that the revolution starts at home and involves treating women – including 'their' women – differently. Women saw that if this was how the revolution was going to be, then it wasn't a revolution for women, and that 'the revolution that allows me to be me, to laugh and to think for myself – well, I've got to do it differently, and do it myself.'[9]

The importance of May '68 for women, then, was double-edged. It acted as a catalyst, helped bring them to a new awareness of their needs and desires. Women glimpsed the possibility for change, but at the same time they realised that the kind of change they wanted to see would not emerge from a male-dominated revolution, and that they would have to take charge of it themselves. And the cry of men students who interrupted one of the first women-only meetings at the University of Paris at Vincennes in 1970 – 'power lies at the tip of the phallus' – merely served to reinforce this awareness.

When the MLF emerged as an autonomous movement, over the next year or two, its ambivalent relationship to the May Movement was clear in what it adopted and what it rejected. In one sense, the women's movement continued the spirit of May '68, adopting its spontaneous actions and its rejection of leadership and organisation. In another sense, the women militants began to develop a new, completely different theory of oppression and exploitation, which placed gender squarely in the centre of their analysis; they looked at their own oppression, their own exploitation, not only in the perspective of capitalism but in that of patriarchy; they reinstated the value of everyday experience, casting aside claims to objectivity and reasserting the importance of experience as lived and felt by women. In practice too, women militants felt the need to reassess the styles and procedures of mixed groups with which they had felt uncomfortable and dissatisfied.

The account of the early days of the MLF that follows relies heavily on the words of the women who were there: using their reminiscences, autobiographies as well as the articles and tracts that were published then, plus the large number of publications that appeared from 1978 onwards, celebrating the first ten years of the MLF, a picture can be drawn of the more visible aspects of the movement, and its evolution can be roughly charted.[10]

1970

Even before 1970, groups were meeting: mixed groups or women-only groups, based at a university or in one neighbourhood, with a Marxist, a Maoist or no orientation, but wanting to discuss and analyse what it meant to be a woman in capitalist society. These groups sometimes adopted names – the *Petites Marguerites*, the *Polymorphes Perverses*, the *Oreilles Vertes* and many more. Many women, whether in one of these groups or not, came together for debates, which turned into regular open meetings, held at the Beaux-Arts school in Paris. At these meetings, chaos and good humour rather than clarity and order prevailed. Instead of someone in the chair, a pre-registered order of speakers, a motion to be discussed and a vote to be taken, at MLF meetings nobody knew quite what was going on. This unstructured format, a reaction against the rigid procedures of male-dominated political meetings, met with mixed response. Some women found it invigorating, others found it irritating. One woman wrote bluntly that 'every time I went to a general assembly, I wondered what I was doing there.' But another wrote: 'it was magnificent, invigorating. You didn't know what was going on, you couldn't really see anything . . . but still, there was a liveliness, a joy, that I had never seen anywhere else.'

As well as small group meetings and large general assemblies, there were a number of events designed to bring the MLF into the public eye. In August 1970, several women went to the Arc de Triomphe and placed a wreath on the Tomb of the Unknown Soldier dedicated to one more unknown than the soldier – his wife. They were promptly arrested and later released. It was at this event that the name *Mouvement de Libération des Femmes* was first used to describe feminists in France, used by the media in its reporting of the event and taken directly from the American Women's Liberation Movement. One newspaper said that there were 3000 members of the French chapter of this movement; another described the women as 'petticoat guerillas' and printed a photograph of the women (in which it was clear that none wore a skirt).[11]

In November 1970, feminists interrupted a conference on 'Woman' organised by the magazine *Elle*, upsetting the self-congratulatory atmosphere of the conference in which mostly male celebrities and a few women talked as experts about women's condition. A questionnaire had been circulated by *Elle* prior to the conference so that a comprehensive portrait of the French Woman could be painted, using the answers of thousands of women as uncontestable evidence. Women from the MLF distributed their own questionnaire and showed exactly what they thought of the *Elle* effort, by turning some of the original questions on their heads. For instance, the question: 'Do you think that women are more, equally or less able than men to drive a car' was replaced by 'In your opinion, do double X chromosomes contain the genes of double declutching?' There were also additions to the questionnaire, such as: 'Do you wear make up: (a) out of self-loathing? (b) to look less like yourself and more like what you are expected to look like?' and: 'When a man talks to a woman, should he address (a) her tits and her legs? (b) her arse and her tits? or (c) just her arse?'

As well as these events, designed to shock and startle the public, there were the first feminist publications, written by women and for women. There was first the collection mentioned above, called *Libération des femmes année zéro* and published as a special issue of the journal *Partisans;* and there was the first issue of the feminist newspaper *Le Torchon brûle* (The Burning Rag) published initially as a special issue of the libertarian newspaper *L'Idiot international* (The International Idiot) and later as an autonomous feminist newspaper. *Le Torchon* was published seven times in all over a three-year period, produced each time by a different team of women. The *Torchon's* aim was to reflect the MLF's increasing diversity and share opinions and experiences, to break women's silence, leave an imprint on paper and therefore in history. There was no desire to produce polished journalism, but instead to avoid the division between those who can write and those who read and to encourage women to write whether they thought they could or not. Women wrote about themselves, their life histories, their anger and their feelings about the MLF. The texts are often difficult to read, as they lack structure and coherence – thoughts ramble, ideas are repeated, sentences are unfinished. The reader's expectations are constantly arrested in the process of reading and then suspended; there was no censorship, no editorial policy, no columns on the page, no rubrics; on the page, drawings, pictures, handwriting and typescripts, all in many colours, jostled for space. Articles were written anonymously, both to show that names be-

Cover of *Le Torchon brûle* No. 1

longed to fathers and husbands and to avoid the creation of a star system; the problems that arose from this anonymity did not appear until a little later on, when the practice was abandoned in favour of first names, and still later, in favour of first and surnames.

1971

More groups formed and there were as many feminisms as there were groups: the *autogestionnaire* (self-management) socialist feminist group, the *Cercle Elisabeth Dmitriev*; the *Gouines Rouges* (Red Dykes); groups in colleges and factories, consciousness-raising groups and study groups, groups for this and groups for that. Feminists went to support women on strike at a hat factory in Troyes, some wanting to spread a particular feminist message, others simply wanting to demonstrate solidarity between women; women in far-Left mixed groups began to speak out against the sexism of their male comrades and to organise separately as feminists; support was given to the under-age single pregnant girls who were protesting at the conditions in which they were forced to live at a hostel in a Paris suburb.

The event that dominated media attention to feminism was the publication in the weekly news magazine *Le Nouvel Observateur* on 5 April 1971 of a Manifesto signed by 343 women, declaring that they had had illegal abortions. The text read:

A million women abort every year in France. They do it under dangerous conditions because they are condemned to clandestinity, although, when done under medical supervision, this operation is extremely simple.
No-one ever mentions these millions of women. I declare that I am one of them. I declare that I have had an abortion.
Just as we demand free access to contraception, we demand freedom of abortion.

The women who signed included the best known figures of stage, screen and intellectual life, with Simone de Beauvoir at the head. This marked the beginning of the campaign for free legal abortion on demand, which was the biggest mobilising issue of the MLF in the early 1970s. After the publication of the Manifesto, the association

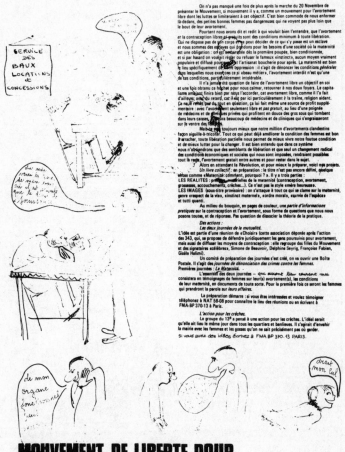

On n'a pas manqué une fois de plus après la marche du 20 Novembre de présenter le Mouvement, si mouvement il y a, comme un mouvement pour l'avortement libre dont les luttes se limiteraient à cet objectif. C'est bien commode de nous enfermer là-dedans, des petites bonnes femmes pas dangereuses qui ne voyent pas plus loin que le bout de leur avortement.

Pourtant nous avons dit et redit à qui voulait bien l'entendre, que l'avortement et la contraception libres et gratuits sont des conditions minimum à toute libération. Qui ne dispose pas de son corps ne peut décider de ce qui s'y passe est un esclave et nous sommes des esclaves qui pondons pour les besoins d'une société où la maternité est une obligation : on est embarquée dès la première poupée, bien conditionnée, et si par hasard on voulait régler ou refuser le fameux «instinct», aucun moyen vraiment populaire et diffusé pour ça. L'artisanat boucherie pour après. La maternité est bien le lieu spécifiquement de notre oppression : il s'agit de dénoncer les conditions générales dans lesquelles nous exerçons ce p'sbeau métier, l'avortement interdit n'est qu'une de ces conditions, particulièrement intolérable.

Il n'a jamais été question de faire de l'avortement libre un objectif en soi et une fois obtenu ce hochet pour nous calmer, retourner à nos doux foyers. Le capitalisme ambiant finira bien par nous l'accorder, cet avortement libre, comme il l'a fait d'ailleurs, avec du retard, car il est par ici particulièrement à la traîne, religion aidant. Ce n'est remis pas du tout en question, ça lui fait même une source de profit supplémentaire : avec l'avortement seulement libre et pas gratuit, au lieu d'une poignée de médecins et de cliniques privées qui profitent en douce des gros sous qui tombent dans leurs caisses, il y aura beaucoup de médecins et de cliniques qui s'engraisseront sur le ventre des femmes.

Mais ça vaut toujours mieux que notre million d'avortements clandestins façon aiguille-à-tricoter. Tout ce qui peut déjà améliorer la condition des femmes est bon à arracher, toute libération partielle nous permet de mieux vivre notre foutue condition et de mieux lutter pour la changer. Il est bien entendu que dans ce système nous n'obtiendrons que des semblants de libération et que seul un changement radical des conditions économiques et sociales qui nous sont imposées, rendraient possibles tout le reste, l'avortement gratuit entre autres et pour mieux le préparer, voici nos projets.

Un livre collectif : en préparation : le titre n'est pas encore défini, quelque chose comme «Maternité: comment, pourquoi ? ». Il y a trois parties :
LES REALITES : premières merveilles de la maternité (contraception, avortement, grossesse, accouchement, crèches...). Ce n'est pas le style «mère heureuse».
LES IMAGES (sous-titre provisoire) : on s'attaque à tout ce qui se clame sur la maternité, genre «respect de la vie», «instinct maternel», «ordre moral», «survie de l'espèce» et tutti quanti.
Au milieu du bouquin, en pages de couleur, une partie d'informations pratiques sur la contraception et l'avortement, sous forme de questions que nous nous posons toutes, et de réponses. Pas question de dissocier la théorie de la pratique.

Des actions :
Les deux journées de la mutualité.
L'idée est partie d'une réunion de «Choisir» (cette association déponée après l'action des 343, qui, se propose de défendre juridiquement les gens poursuivis pour avortement, mais aussi de diffuser les moyens de contraception : elle regroupe des filles du Mouvement et des signataires célèbres, Simone de Beauvoir, Delphine Seyrig, Françoise Fabien, Gisèle Halimi).

Un comité de préparation des journées s'est créé, on va ouvrir une Boîte Postale. Il s'agit des journées de dénonciation des crimes contre les femmes. Premières journées : La Maternité.

L'essentiel des deux journées – qui auront lieu courant mai – consistera en témoignages de femmes sur leur(s) avortement(s), les conditions de leur maternité, en documents de toute sorte. Pour la première fois ce seront les femmes qui prendront la parole sur leurs affaires.

La préparation démarre : si vous êtes intéressées et voulez témoigner téléphonez à NAT 58-08 pour connaître le lieu des réunions ou en écrivant à FMA-BP 370-13 à Paris.

L'action pour les crèches.
Le groupe du 13e a pensé à une action pour les crèches. L'idéal serait qu'elle ait lieu le même jour dans tous les quartiers et banlieues. Il s'agirait d'envahir la mairie avec les femmes et les gosses qu'on ne sait précisément pas où garder.
Si vous avez des idées écrivez à FMA BP 370.13 PARIS.

MOUVEMENT DE LIBERTE POUR L'AVORTEMENT

Le Torchon brûle No. 3 p. 23

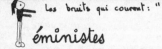

Les bruits qui courent: "les Féministes sont bottées et casquées"

éministes

Voici une Féministe casquée →

Voici une Féministe ← bottée

évolutionnaires

On parle beaucoup dans le Mouvement des Féministes Révolutionnaires. Outre que celles qui reçoivent cette étiquette ne la revendiquent pas toutes lesdites « F.R. » tellement d'options, qu'il est difficile de parler de « ligne générale ».

Néanmoins, on essaye d'exposer ici l'histoire de ce groupe et ce que les femmes qui y ont participé en ont dégagé.

Nous pensons que cette mise au point permettra de mieux comprendre où nous en sommes et de ne pas nous figer dans des images plaquées de l'extérieur, souvent très fantaisistes.

LES FEMINISTES REVOLUTIONNAIRES (première partie)

C'était au début de ce qui devait plus tard — de ce qui était déjà connu sous le nom de Mouvement de libération des femmes.

Un soir d'octobre 1970 à une assemblée générale, des filles se déclarèrent Féministes Révolutionnaires. Pourquoi Féministes, pourquoi Révolutionnaires, pourquoi ce dire ?

— Pour nous, féministes, ça voulait dire :

D'ABORD POUR LES FEMMES. Cela semblerait évident dans un mouvement de femmes mais ça ne l'était pas pour tout le monde. La mauvaise conscience de femmes sortaient sous la forme d'une compulsion à se culpabiliser sur la lutte des classes, à l'opposer à la lutte des femmes comme si celle-ci allait à l'encontre de la lutte des classes, et contrairement, à vouloir faire rentrer de gré ou de force la lutte des femmes dans les schémas de la lutte des classes.

— Féministes ça voulait dire :

POUR LES FEMMES ET AVEC TOUTES LES FEMMES. Ce n'était pas évident pour tout le monde non plus. Certaines disaient qu'il n'y avait pas de « NOUS » des femmes, et pourtant c'est bien en tant que femmes qu'elles étaient réunies. Elles excluaient les bourgeoises des femmes opprimées, et pourtant elles se disaient bourgeoises.

« Nous », on sentait bien qu'il y avait un NOUS des femmes, que « femme » était notre première identité, avant prolétaire ou bourgeoise. Mieux, nous sentions que jusque dans leurs identités de classe différentes les femmes avaient un point commun : c'était de les avoir à travers un homme (le père ou le mari).

Parmi nous, certaines pensaient que cela faisait des femmes une classe, d'autres une caste, et beaucoup s'en fichaient : pensaient simplement que toutes les femmes ont quelque chose en commun, et que c'était de ce commun qu'il fallait partir.

Féministes donc d'abord parce que ça veut dire : « D'abord pour les femmes. » C'est ce que ça a toujours voulu dire depuis un siècle pour qui le terme existe.

Nous nous sentions en liaison avec les femmes pour elles « qui ont existé » avant nous, lutté avant nous. Quelque chose plus n'allait pas de soi. Les autres le refusaient parce que féministes c'est péjoratif, parce que ces ancêtres étaient réformistes. Mais ce n'est pas pour ça que le terme est devenu péjoratif. Ou il a rendu péjoratif et pourquoi ? Le refuser pour nous c'était concourir avec ceux qui ont passé sous silence ou déformé la lutte des femmes, avec ceux qui ont ridiculisé les femmes qui osaient lutter pour elles-mêmes, avec ceux qui ont fait de la suffragette l'image-épouvantail qu'on brandissait devant les velléités de révolte.

Nous n'allions pas abandonner ces femmes, leur revolte, la nôtre. Nous n'allions pas à courir en courbant la tête sous les huées, à la recherche d'un terme qui conviendrait à ces messieurs. Quelque mot que nous trouvions ils nous le renverront sali. C'est notre révolte elle-même qui est sale pour eux, qui est « pour eux » réactionnaire, réformiste et petite bourgeoise, comme les « bonnes femmes » et leurs histoires, cachées, couchées !

Si nous revendiquions toute cette femme, parce que le terme ? Et si nous commençons à reculer devant l'injure jusqu'où irions-nous ? Pour nous c'était important, c'était le début du renversement de leur ordre et de leur loi que de nous dénommer du terme de leur dérision et de leur opprobre : féministes. Ce n'est pas grâce au pelées et aux tondues du courage « Féministes Révolutionnaires » non, que le terme a commencé à changer de sens. Mais comme il grandit, que le mouvement existe, qu'il est vivant, qu'il commence à être grand, qu'il est partout, et qu'il est pour les femmes, on l'appelle féministe et on rit de moins en moins.

— Pourquoi révolutionnaire ?

Révolutionnaire ça voulait dire pour nous « radicales ». Pas d'amélioration des conditions de détention, mais tout chambarder.

Ça voulait dire aussi que la lutte des femmes si elle est menée jusqu'au bout, jusqu'à la destruction totale de l'ordre patriarcal, remet en question les fondements même de la société, donc en fiche un coup à pas mal d'autres choses. Par exemple on n'avait pas d'inquiétude de « s'intégrer » dans le capitalisme et de risquer d'opprimer les ouvriers à notre tour c'était, c'est toujours la vision d'horreur qui se présente en premier à pas mal de filles quand elles entendaient parler du Mouvement, et à tous les mecs ; comme on sait par le nombre de femmes qui oppriment des ouvriers, c'est en effet un danger très menaçant et réel.

Parce que : vous imaginez une société capitaliste sans famille ? (Même Hector Malot ne pourrait pas.)

— Révolutionnaire c'était pas — surtout pas — une façon de se raccrocher aux « révolutionnaires » — vous savez ces fils de famille qui ont reçu en héritage le bien suprême, la Révolution avec un grand R, et l'octroient parcimonieusement aux masses méritantes — mais, disent-ils, il n'y a plus beaucoup de masses méritantes, « ils ont la télé ces salauds, l'ouvrier n'a plus de respect, il s'embourgeoise, une voiture c'est tout pour la conscience de classe », tandis que les fils de famille, eux, ont une conscience qui sait d'une autre classe, elle, qui résiste au confort, ce n'est pas eux que leurs frigidaires empêchent de penser juste, et pour tout le monde qui plus est il faut dire qu'ils ont de l'entraînement le confort c'est une question d'habitude (penser pour les autres aussi).

Donc on ne voulait pas faire partie des privilèges, des attributaires de la Révolution, on ne voulait pas de part au partage de leurs « programmes de transition », ni des querelles : l'U.R.S.S. est-elle un Etat ouvrier dégénéré ou un Etat capitaliste d'Etat ? Si c'est ça l'essentiel eh bien on préfère donner (comme dit Simone) dans l'inessentiel.

Révolutionnaires : on prenait en charge notre révolution — on ne pensait pas que c'était une pierre qu'on apportait à l'édifice commun, ni qu'on puiserait nos « revendications » au grand livre blanc pour les « révolutionnaires » on l'ouvrent au matin du grand soir et se disent : « Tiens voyons ce qu...

veulent les bonnes femmes. » On ne voulait pas faire partie de la Grande Révolution Socialiste parce qu'on n'y croit pas. On ne croit pas qu'il existe un schéma valable pour tout le monde pensé par quelques-uns et appliqué par quelques autres. On ne croit aux fronts principaux et secondaires, ni aux contradictions principales et secondaires. Mais il y a l'oppression — non —, les oppressions, multiples, combinées, tout le monde à la fois oppresseur et opprimé.

On croit que la meilleure façon de comprendre les autres opprimés, c'est de lutter contre notre oppression, et la même chose pour eux.

Révolutionnaires ça voulait dire justement que des femmes luttant pour elles-mêmes ça risque de donner des idées aux autres opprimés, comme les Noirs luttant pour eux-mêmes ont donné des idées aux femmes. Tous les opprimés luttant en même temps — et pas sagement à tour de rôle — eux-mêmes, à partir d'eux et pour eux — et pas à partir d'un schéma universel pour l'homme universel — ça risque de foutre un coup à la grande révolution, ça risque d'attaquer sérieusement l'oppression de tous les côtés et là où elle est, ça risque de faire la révolution.

— Pourquoi le dire ?

On aurait préféré pas. On aurait préféré que ça aille de soi, en fait, ça nous semblait invraisemblable d'avoir à préciser à l'intérieur d'un mouvement de femmes qu'on était d'abord pour les femmes. Mais c'était ainsi. A l'époque ça n'allait pas de soi. Cette question coinçait tout. On ne pouvait plus travailler, on avait fait la preuve qu'on s'en engueulait stériles.

Alors à la rentrée les filles qui étaient d'accord là-dessus ont décidé de se réunir ensemble pour pouvoir reprendre le travail et la discussion.

Les féministes étaient plus et moins que cet accord minimal.

Plus parce que ce n'était qu'une base de départ, à partir de laquelle en travaillant ensemble, on développait des façons communes d'aborder des questions précises de la lutte. Moins parce que d'autres facteurs jouaient dans la composition du groupe : le hasard de la visite des groupes les filles qui arrivaient, les affinités.

Vers janvier 1971, si le groupe Féministes Révolutionnaires s'est dissous, il y a bien entendu autant d'interprétations de cette fin qu'il y a de filles à l'avoir vécue.

Il y avait des tensions comme dans tous les groupes, à tous les niveaux : on n'avait pas toutes la même façon de concevoir les priorités, les centres d'intérêts, les façons de travailler, les modes d'action. On n'avait pas toutes la même conception du groupe, de sa fonction. Il ne servait pas les mêmes buts, n'occupait pas la même place pour toutes, on n'avait pas toutes le même rapport affectif au groupe et aux autres filles du groupe. Et c'est en fonction de tout ça aussi que les explications de sa fin divergent.

Mais ce qui a permis à ces tensions et ces divergences de mener à l'éclatement, c'est la raison d'être fondamentale du groupe.

Il s'était créé surtout en réaction à l'opposition extérieure et à l'impossibilité de discuter avec les gauchistes. Or à la fin de l'hiver il est apparu que le Mouvement tout entier était devenu plus pratique, sinon dans son discours, certes sur les femmes. Il est devenu possible pour nous de travailler partout. L'accord général qui nous avait réunies, ressurgit maintenant tout le Mouvement. La pression extérieure qui nous avait réunies avait disparu, et c'est non pas ce qui a motivé, mais c'est la condition objective qui a permis la dissolution du groupe. → Suite P. 9

FEMINISTES OUI !

Y a encore un bémol.

Le groupe Musique n'a pas de local pour faire du bruit, beaucoup de bruit même, car on sort notre batterie des grands jours. Même que la fanfare ne fanfaronne plus vaillamment faute de moyens : instruments à vent et local. Alors, on en a ras-le-bol de faire de la zizique dans notre coin, on sent nos talents diminuer de jour en jour, on se lève la nuit pour pleurer et se console comme on peut...

Les musiciennes latentes et battantes peuvent rencontrer d'autres musiciennes vacantes qui les accueilleront avec tambours et trompettes 11 rue Blomet, 5 étage à gauche.

Une femme de Gien (Loiret) désire rencontrer d'autres femmes. Contacter Judith, 5 rue Bernard-Palissy.

Choisir (Choice) was formed to defend the signatories in case of prosecution. *Choisir* began with a clear focus on the abortion issue but gradually developed into a major reform-based organisation, moving from this single issue to broader attention to reforms for women in every domain of social and political life. The dominant figure in *Choisir*, lawyer Gisèle Halimi, is now a member of the French parliament as an independent candidate affiliated to the Socialist party.

From as early on as 1970 and 1971, splits were appearing between women in the MLF: it was not all sisterhood and harmony. Diverging analyses of women's oppression and ways of acting as feminists were emerging and proving to be obstacles in the path of collective action. However, these differences were on the whole absorbed and accepted by women and did not turn into hostility and constant conflict until later on.

1972

Feminists continued to support women on strike in different parts of France; the general assemblies continued; new groups were formed, more texts were written. Public events included a demonstration on the Champs Elysées against Mother's Day ('celebrated one day of the year, exploited the rest'); and a two-day meeting in Paris about crimes against women, which attracted over 5000 women. Later in the year, the trial of 4 women accused of procuring an abortion for the 11-year old daughter of one of them, at Bobigny (a Paris suburb), brought abortion to the foreground again.[12]

1973

In this year, a publishing project called simply *des femmes* (women/ of women/some women) was founded by one group *Psychanalyse et Politique* (commonly known as *Psych et Po*); a mixed movement was formed to fight the abortion campaign, called the *Mouvement pour la Libération de l'Avortement* (Movement for the Liberation of Abortion – to which 'and Contraception' was added, forming the acronym MLAC); events included a women's fair organised by another group,

15

the *Féministes Révolutionnaires* (Revolutionary Feminists); *Le Torchon brûle* was taken to court for obscenity after printing photographs in the newspaper of women's genitals, to illustrate an article called 'The power of the cunt'; a feminist journal, *les Cahiers du GRIF*, (The GRIF Notebooks) was founded in Brussels.

1974

The *Féministes Révolutionnaires* seemed to become more fragmented, with many specific initiatives begun by women who had been involved with them – some founded an information centre for women, others formed a group to work specifically on sexism in legislation, still others opened a shelter for battered women; several feminist newspapers were started, replacing *Le Torchon brûle* which no longer appeared. Different groups now put out their own journals, expressing their own feminism rather than expressing the differences and contradictions within the MLF in one 'Movement' newspaper. In 1974 too, women who wanted to explore feminism from the perspective of its relationship to the Left formed a specific 'current' of the MLF and held a national meeting for women with similar preoccupations; and *Psych et Po* opened the first of their *des femmes* bookshops in Paris.

1975

This was declared International Women's Year by the United Nations, while feminists cried 'co-option'. Rather than celebrating, feminist attention was on violence against women, on rape cases and the way that rape trials were conducted, on prostitution and pornography.

*   *   *

The second half of the decade saw some campaigns continue, the by now familiar pattern of groups forming and dissolving, an increase in feminist publications, the first court case involving *Psych et Po* against other women, splits between groups and between individual women. In 1978, women began to organise as feminists in the French Communist Party (PCF) and in the Socialist Party (PS); and in 1979, *Psych et Po* registered as their own property the name *Mouvement de Libération des Femmes* and the logo MLF, which now became their company title and trademark. While this conflict dominated the internal life of the MLF, individual and collective initiatives continued and feminism began to make inroads into higher education and research, feminist networks became more visible.

This gallop through only some of the actions and events of the MLF's first few years shows the energy and anger that went with the initial actions as women who were feeling uncomfortable with what was said to be women's role and nature realised that they were not misfits suffering from a problem with no name, but shared a common oppression which could be named and analysed as a political situation. The energy and anger was directed in a number of ways, and the diversity of projects and attitudes has always been part of the richness of the MLF's life, as it is in women's movements everywhere. Yet the differences did not always live side by side in mutual acceptance and there were tensions and conflict from very early on.

One of the earliest contentious issues was precisely about how the MLF should appear, how far it wanted to be publicly visible and identified with the 'spectacular' actions such as the Arc de Triomphe wreath, or how far it was felt that invisibility was preferable while the MLF was developing its own analyses of women's oppression. 'We want to be anonymous, underground, like moles,' said *Psych et Po*, while the *Féministes Révolutionnaires* wanted to burst into the world with as much noise and attention as possible. The split between these two groups meant that two very different approaches to feminism were emerging, soon complemented by a third approach, that of the 'class struggle current'.

When talking about these approaches in the MLF, women often refer to them as 'currents' or 'tendencies', as each approach corresponded more or less to three separate groupings, who met separately, thought and acted differently and produced separate publications. However, it would be wrong to think that they developed in separate parallel ways: the situation in the early 1970s was much more fluid than this suggests: there were agreements as well as violent quarrels; aspects of their analyses overlapped as well as differed; each approach evolved at different rhythms over the decade; and women who identified as feminists frequently identified with neither one group nor another, or with several at different times. The experience of Françoise Picq demonstrates how women were not limited in their actions and ideas to one 'current' or another. She writes:

> I can't locate my own experience in any one current . . . At the beginning, there was a great degree of flexibility, and everyone participated in her own way in the collective events . . . it didn't matter who initiated and organised them . . . While certain currents were dominant here or there, none was exclusive. For instance, I was never involved in any of the groups started by the *Féministes Révolutionnaires*, but I did do some things with them, such as produce one issue of *Le Torchon brûle*; I never felt part of the *tendance lutte des classes* (class struggle current) although I was active in a mixed political group and did participate in local groups started by them; I went to *Psych et Po* meetings although I didn't agree with the group and broke with them in 1973. And yet the problems I've had and still have with these currents have never made me feel like an outsider.[13]

All the groups had to confront the same problems; questions of alliances with political parties, attitudes to men, analyses of women's sexuality, formed part of the concerns of all the groups. It was the varying responses to these issues that caused the early conflicts and led to the forming of the separate currents.

The first of these disagreements was over the relation of women's struggle to the class struggle. As with feminists all over the world, French feminists disagreed over the roots of women's oppression: whether it was capitalism or patriarchy (or both) which was to blame. Even among women who retained close links with the Left, there has been divergence over the relative importance of the two struggles and the ways in which they intersect.[14] For feminists, it became a question of identity: whether they identified first as socialists/communists or as feminists, and whether women identified first as women and second as working-class or middle-class or vice versa; or whether, indeed, the entire concept of class had to be reformulated in order to account for gender in a satisfactory way.

Contradictory positions appeared among women who focused on this question: 'Women's liberation is a specific struggle' wrote one group, 'the class struggle is a necessary part of it, but isn't enough,' while another group wrote 'we must work to unite working women, strengthen their class consciousness . . . and contribute in this way to the unity of the working class and to workers' control of women's struggle.'

Later in the decade, feminists in political parties of the Left, which each claimed to be more-feminist-than-thou, experienced the difficulty of marrying the two struggles. The women who founded the feminist *Elles Voient Rouge* (Women See Red) collective in the PCF in 1979 wrote that:

Feminism has brought out a new contradiction in our own practice: we have to define ourselves not only in opposition to capitalism but also in opposition to the sexism we are subjected to, including the sexism of our 'little friends' in the party.

These women went on to argue against trying to fit women into a Marxist class analysis, which some feminists had been unsuccessfully attempting to do, and in favour of 'understanding the double oppression/exploitation of patriarchy and capitalism working together.'

Other feminists saw the problem in terms of situating women as a class. Again, there was disagreement: 'We do not believe that women form a class in the Marxist sense: we have to recognise that women are divided amongst themselves' said one neighbourhood group (the *Group du 12e Arrondissement*). The *Féministes Révolutionnaires* thought otherwise: '. . . we felt that there was a collective "we" of women – that "woman" was our primary identity before working class or middle class.' They acknowledged that this collective pronoun for women was more a goal than a present reality, was something that had to be worked for. The radical feminist journal *Questions féministes* (Feminist Issues), on the other hand, affirmed that women did form a social class based on gender, and defined their feminist politics from this: women form a class whose oppression is justified by the dominant group (men) using biological determinism, women's bodies, as the rationale. For the *Questions Féministes* collective, positing women as a class was the first condition of all feminist struggle.

The theoretical implications of this debate may be rich, in that the concept of class is scrutinised by some and recast by others in the light of a new recognition of the difference of gendered experience, but it has had difficult practical consequences. It has meant blockages

19

over strategy, problems over the context of actions and quarrels over the perspective in which actions are perceived. Feminists who have wanted to maintain a political allegiance to a party have found themselves in untenable situations and have had to deny either their feminism or their party allegiance – usually the latter.

The second area of conflict that has existed in France since the early 1970s, is over the existence or not of a specifically feminine difference.[15] The issue is symptomatic of the incompatible approaches in the MLF to the whole question of women's oppression and women's liberation. The notion of difference, the exploration of the unconscious and the positing of an autonomous feminine identity created with no reference to men and beginning at the level of the unconscious has led to fascinating theoretical work, some of which will be discussed in Chapters 2 and 5. It has however had problematic political and structural implications for the MLF itself and for its relation with the non-feminist world.

Many feminists believe that men and women perceive and experience the world, experience their bodies and express their experience in fundamentally different ways. There are different degrees of this position. For instance, the newspaper *Histoires d'elles* (Her Stories) hoped that it would transmit experience through 'women's lenses', deriving their positions from acknowledgement of different life experience rather than from an essentialist notion. The literary journal *Sorcières* (Sorceresses/Witches) felt differently. In their first editorial, the editorial collective showed that they thought that women had a different voice: 'this other voice which we are beginning to hear in the cracks of the socio-symbolic order, the unsaid, the nonmeaning, the repressed, the holes that this voice is tearing in the fabric of masculine discourse.'

The most developed questioning about difference has taken place in the group *Psych et Po*, for whom it constitutes the heart of the revolutionary problem. They describe their 'work' as the search to 'get away from reproducing masculinity.' Masculinity controls even at the level of the unconscious, and women operate within the confines of masculine unconscious structures and have been turned into misogynists, despising their own womanhood. To free themselves from this internalised oppression, each woman must, according to *Psych et Po*, work to 'chase the phallus from her head'. Only once this has been accomplished will women be able to discover and cherish their difference.

Critiques of difference have appeared in many non-*Psych et Po* journals and newspapers. *Questions Féministes* has led a systematic attack on the notion of difference, calling it a biological justification of domination:

'difference' is, historically, the same thing as maintaining women in an inferior position . . . this notion of equality in difference does not hold up . . . all it is, is an ideology of domination whose goal is to hide that domination.[16]

For *Questions Féministes* and women who defined themselves as radical feminists, difference constituted a dangerous political concept with an idealist base, assuming that there is something that exists in women, a relation to language, an identity, that is unmediated by the social. The ambiguity of the term 'difference' is also pointed out:

On the one hand, difference means a number of anatomical-physiological givens, and on the other, socio-psychological phenomena. This allows a double game to be played, consciously or not, and the notion can be used in one register or the other, depending on the time and the need.[17]

Questions Féministes obviously doesn't question the self-evidence of biological differences between men and women, but the editorial collective rejects the way that certain attributes are assigned to masculinity and others to femininity, which, they say, locks men and women into roles and behaviour incorrectly and unjustly defined as natural. They therefore reject any suggestion of innate differences and hold that speaking of difference is simply 'noting the effects of a power relation'.

La Revue d'en face,[18] another mostly radical feminist journal, attacks difference on several counts, including the loss of individuality that occurs when all women are fused into a harmonious whole: 'I used to be me and now I'm a Woman.'[19] This loss of individuality was evident within *Psych et Po*, and one ex-participant wrote how she noticed 'a stupefying transformation' as women in the group adopted the words and ideas of Antoinette Fouque, who led the group. Nadja Ringart wrote that 'women who behaved and spoke in their own different ways, gradually turned into parrots, resolutely repeating their master's words.'[20]

Psyche et Po, concentrating on the symbolic nature of women's oppression and aiming at the creation of a feminine future, also developed a group practice that was alien to other feminisms. What began as difference of opinion became a gulf between this group and all others which is as impossible to cross in 1985 as it was in 1977, the year in which *des femmes* went to court for the first time.

A third area of conflict has created a further gulf between feminist groups. This is the question of heterosexuality and lesbianism. Female sexuality has been an issue of central importance to feminists since the birth of the MLF. At first, lesbians felt excluded, repressed by heterosexual women in the MLF. Then, many heterosexual feminists felt that a radical hierarchy was being set up, and lesbianism was held up as a subversive practice to which all feminists, to be properly radical, should aspire. Some women have found that lesbianism is the logical conclusion to a political analysis which identifies men as oppressors (as radical feminism does clearly, and 'class struggle' feminism does circuitously and reluctantly); other women have struggled with this contradiction in their lives, trying to reconcile politics and sexuality within the context of heterosexual relations.

As forms of sexuality, heterosexuality and lesbianism have not caused rifts in the MLF. The quarrel is precisely over the claim that lesbianism and heterosexuality are not forms of sexuality, but are political strategies, and that lesbianism is the only acceptable political position for feminists particularly for radical feminists who identify women and men as class enemies. Women supporting the radical lesbian position have now chosen to organise separately from the MLF, rejecting identification as feminist. In one tract setting out their political position, the collective for a Lesbian Front wrote in 1981:

> Just as we believed in calling ourselves feminists because . . . of
> the historical content of this notion, because we want to reassert
> our solidarity with all the women resistors of the past who
> cleared the path for us, so we believe in calling ourselves lesbians
> . . . to affirm our community with all the resistors – 'dykes',
> 'homosexual women', . . . who show by their lives that it is
> impossible for them to submit in their daily lives to the private
> power relations between men and women.

The question of lesbianism as a political position rather than a sexuality was not new but took on a particularly public and angry shape in 1980 and 1981, focusing on the journal *Questions feministes* which had reopened this debate by publishing two articles (Monique Wittig's 'Straight Thinking' and Emmanuèle de Lessep's 'Heterosexuality and Feminism') in the February 1980 issue.[21] A movement-wide debate began again leading to a split in the *Questions feministes* collective. The collective wanted an issue of *Qf* to be produced in order to set out the terms of the debate and explain to the readership – which went beyond the limits of the MLF – exactly what was going on. But the radical feminist group in the collective, without informing either the publisher or the radical lesbians, decided not to go ahead with this issue and, in the absence of any clear explanation, the radical lesbians wrote a 'letter to the feminist movement' which they distributed at a meeting held on International Women's Day at the Salle Wagram on March 8 1981. The radical lesbians assert that 'the political lesbian current that was emerging, far from contradicting radical feminism, was in fact developing it.' In the first *Qf* editorial, when the theory of sex classes was set out, the practical aspects of resistance to the oppression exercised by the class of men had not been theorised: this is what the radical lesbians aim to do in their writing and to live in their lives. Their attack on hetero-power and hetero-sociality in the 'letter to the feminist movement' is very powerful and deserves some space:

. . . Radical lesbianism is not a 'sexual preference' or only 'liking to live with women'. It is a decisive political choice which is implicit in the analysis of sex class relations based on exploitation and oppression, and which have antagonistic interests. Lesbian political commitment is different from the feminism of 'homosexuals' or 'heterosexuals' because we choose to use the margins of freedom, of manoeuvre that the patriarchal system leaves us, to fight it at its roots . . .

The lesbian choice is *mobilisation,* in a *visible* collective movement, and the transfer of all our creative powers, both intellectual and emotional, to women, because we all have the same class interests. Far from wanting to carve out spaces for ourselves in a hetero-patriarchal society which objectivizes, oppresses and kills women, we want to fight the mechanisms of its power.

The lesbian choice is *awareness* that male violence against

23

women is at work everywhere, especially in 'private' life, with its traps of emotional attachment or heterosexual 'desire' . . . It is decision turned *into act* to use certain social conditions which allow us to reject the material and psychological privileges that men give to those women who are still under the illusion that, in certain exchanges with the enemy, they can escape their own oppression as women. Heterosexual power . . . is, in our view, a fundamental strategy of patriarchy . . .

The split is one within radical feminism: the political (radical) lesbians are not attacking feminist 'currents' which do not claim to be against the class of men: their analysis is the logical conclusion to the radical feminist argument as it was begun in *Questions féministes*. They say that they are not hostile to heterosexual women, but do not agree with feminists who think that individual men can be saved, that heterosexual relations are a 'terrain for struggle'.

Psych et Po did not share in this quarrel. They rarely use the term 'lesbian', believing that it is negative and indicates deviation from a norm instead of a free sexual option or a practice of solidarity with women. The writer Hélène Cixous who has been closely associated with the group even asserted at a conference in New York that French women did not use the words lesbian or feminist and was angrily contradicted by the other French women present. *Psych et po* prefer to talk about love between women, women together, seeming to concentrate on the sensuality of sisterhood in the group. The group's ideas about forming a women-only space in which true femininity would eventually be able to develop clearly posits female homosexuality as a necessary part of this strategy, but as they explore sexuality rather in terms of psychoanalysis than in terms of a political position, they could not share the framing of the argument about lesbianism with the radical lesbians, whose separatism *Psych et Po* share in practice.

One of the problems connected to this question is not only the substance of the arguments made, but the implications for the MLF's strategy and its insistence on diversity. Radical lesbians, in claiming that their way is the only way, exclude vast numbers of women who are unable or unwilling to make the same choices, and are therefore accused of being divisive of women. They counter this by saying that it is in fact heterosexual women who are divisive. For other feminists, the radical lesbian analysis is a denial of the MLF's mutual tolerance that accepts disagreements but would never set up one position that would apparently be more feminist, or better feminism, than another. The radical lesbians were accused of being as monolithic in their approach as *Psych et Po*.

These quarrels and differences, internal to the MLF, have sharpened feminist focus on the MLF's development and turned it inwards rather than outwards, which frequently gives the impression that the MLF lives its own life regardless of what is going on around it. This is of course not so. However, before turning to connections between feminism and its French context to show the complex nature of the interaction, and the varying degrees of permeability to outside influences and changing circumstances, I want to analyse more closely the different approaches that dominated the MLF through most of the first decade. Again I must stress that these approaches although dominant, did not sum up the full life of the MLF, and the description and analysis that follows should be read with the MLF's changing contours and fluctuating preoccupations in mind.

LES TENDANCES CONTRE LE MOUVEMENT

Ce texte a été écrit en juillet 74 ; il est paru dans Libération amputé (censuré) de sa partie sur l'A.G. du « MLF ». Depuis ce temps les média préfèrent aux femmes du « M.L.F. » toutes les couleuves des hommes malabars de l'Année multi-nationale de « LA » Femme.

Les média, autant par leur manque de rigueur pour s'informer, que par intérêt et idéologie, vendent du « MLF » ; c'est-à-dire une image traditionnelle d'organisation politique parlant sur et au nom des femmes.

En vendant du « MLF », on opère une réduction de la diversité des groupes, tendances, formes de lutte, de leur autonomie et de leur décentralisation au sein du Mouvement de Libération des Femmes.

Ainsi le « MLF »-image devient la meilleure manière de faire taire les femmes en lutte non-étiquetées. Autrement dit, le traditionnel : « quand on n'est pas la femme de Dupont ou Durand, on n'est rien » est devenu, dans le champ de la Libération des Femmes : « quand on n'est pas la, (ou les) femmes du « MLF », on n'est rien ».

AUTRE TRANSFORMATION REDUCTRICE
Depuis peu les média, ne pouvant plus ignorer le phénomène des « tendances » au sein du Mouvement, en font état ; mais elles mentionnent les « tendances » *uniquement*, au détriment des groupes qui se dénomment à partir de projets, de formes de luttes, et de thèmes de réflexion, etc. Bref, au détriment de tous les groupes qui se tiennent délibérément à l'écart des étiquettes aliénantes (fussent-elles « politiques »), du système des « tendances » justement.

Si ces « tendances » sont nommées par les média, au détriment du reste, c'est parce que le système des « tendances » est conforme à l'idée d'organisation ». Simplement l'image d'un « MLF » organisation-homogène s'est déplacée vers l'image d'un « MLF » divisé en plusieurs sous-organisations dénommées « tendances »-ci, « tendances »-ça, etc. L'une et l'autre images tendent à nous réduire à des modèles connus de fonctionnement, des modèles masculins (partis et groupuscules de gauche) aliénants pour nous *toutes* (pour tout le monde, aussi bien).

LE SYSTEME DES « TENDANCES » ET LEUR RECONNAISSANCE AU DETRIMENT DES AUTRES FONCTIONNEMENTS ENTERINENT :
— L'oppression des minorités et des minoritaires ;
— Le fait qu'il faut avoir des pouvoirs reconnus (des privilèges) pour que nous soient octroyés une existence, un droit à la parole, etc.
— Le partage des territoires et des clientèles entre « tendances », et par voie de conséquence des pratiques de prise de pouvoir, d'hégémonie, de plus en plus flagrantes des dites « tendances ».

LES MAUVAISES TENDANCES DES « TENDANCES »

Ce système entérine surtout, et c'est le plus grave, la « spécialisation » croissante de chaque groupe, et sa cristallisation autour de positions extrêmes qui n'ont de sens que les unes par rapport aux autres (l'activité vers l'extérieur ou le travail sur soi, le rejet du système ou son utilisation-détournement, la revendication d'égalité ou celle d'altérité, la lutte légale ou extra-légale, le lien avec les autres luttes révolutionnaires, etc.). Ces options deviennent chacune la spécialité, voire le monopole d'un groupe, de plus en plus crispé sur son « territoire » propre. Le cloisonnement aidant, et l'absence de circulation des femmes entre groupes, font que certaines se retrouvent ainsi préposées *exclusivement* aux actions spectaculaires, d'autres à l'introspection collective, d'autres au travail de masse traditionnel, d'autres encore au réformisme pur et simple. Ces différentes orientations, qui constituent les lignes de force, les pôles permanents et *inséparables* du Mouvement, au lieu de s'équilibrer les unes les autres, d'interagir constamment à l'intérieur de *chaque* groupe, de *chaque* projet d'action, de *chaque* individu, sont localisés sur quelques « tendances ». A partir de là, le mouvement (des femmes, des orientations de lutte, des pratiques et des idées) est remplacé par un système de *blocs* étanches, cloisonnés, parfois ennemis, en tous cas de plus en plus ignorants les uns des autres, et dont chacun revendique pour lui seul la position ou la ligne juste.

Dès lors, toutes les luttes (et les prises) de pouvoir — et de sigle — toutes les hégémonies, tous les impérialismes deviennent possibles.

POUVOIRS ET PRISE DE SIGLE

Les « tendances » reconnues du Mouvement et citées par les médias le sont en fonction de pouvoirs traditionnels valorisés et/ou reconnus par la société patriarcale-capitaliste : pouvoir du spectacle, de la publicité, de l'écriture, pouvoir que donne l'argent, et/ou ou pouvoir de the(o)risation des livres saints (marxistes, psychanalytiques), pouvoir du légalisme, du soutien des hommes, pouvoir du marxisme en tant qu'idée traditionnelle de la politique et de la « lutte des classes ».

Ces réductions successives du Mouvement, d'organisation homogène (premier temps), en « tendances » (deuxième temps) par les médias, c'est alarmant, mais ce n'est pas encore le pire.

Le pire, c'est quand certaines « tendances » du Mouvement se font elles-mêmes complices, pour leur bénéfice, de l'utilisation patronymique, restrictive, centralisatrice, abusive, totalitaire et aliénante du « M.L.F. ».

Il y eut : « Le pouvoir est au bout du Phallus », il y a maintenant, consciemment ou non, dans la pratique de certaines « tendances » : « LE POUVOIR EST AU BOUT DU M.L.F. » !

DEVRONS-NOUS DIRE : « M.L.F.-PHALLUS MEME COMBAT » ?

L'abus du sigle « M.L.F. » est manifeste, entre autres (et on le signale en priorité car malgré une critique parue dans *Libération* rien n'a changé depuis) dans le communiqué annonçant une Assemblée Générale de *toutes* les tendances du M.L.F., les premiers mercredis du mois, rue Guy de la Brosse. La prétention à être la seule A.G. *plus* « M.L.F. » que d'autres, qui fut par les auteurs revendiquée, est inadmissible.

C'est un abus de pouvoir, l'organisation d'une contrainte (à s'y rendre), une monopolisation, un centralisme et de la démagogie publicitaire.

Aucune A.G., en outre, ne peut représenter (ou prétendre représenter) tous les groupes, ou même *toutes* les tendances du Mouvement. Aucun groupe ou tendance (ni même plusieurs d'entre eux) ne peut avoir le monopole de l'Assemblée générale et/ou du sigle « M.L.F. ». Il n'y a pas de « plus » ou de « moins » à M.L.F., selon qu'il s'agisse d'une A.G. de diverses tendances officiellement reconnues du Mouvement, ou d'une A.G. sur un thème ou un projet précis. Ces hiérarchies, outre qu'elles sont absurdes, s'opposent au principe de l'autonomie et de la décentralisation. A quand l'utilisation du sigle à mains levées et par votes, qui la boucleraient aux minorités ? Ne souriez pas d'un M.L.F. en arrivant à ce point de dégradation, c'est la logique contenue dans une utilisation du sigle discernant des « plus » et des « moins » en fonction de la règle des deux unités : du lieu, du temps dont un seul groupe a décidé.

Quand un groupe s'autorise ces pratiques, il en entraîne d'autres à se lancer dans cette course au

Les Femmes s'entêtent p. 8

CHAPTER 2

Currents: diversity and conflict

The *tendance lutte des classes*

Women attracted to the MLF already had experience in mixed political groups, mostly on the extreme Left, and while many women rejected outright their former political practices and their male comrades, those who became involved in the 'class struggle' approach within the MLF did not do this, and were beset by the constant practical problem of how far to retain links with their organisation's thinking and practice, which were often in direct conflict with ideas developing in the MLF.

This approach to feminism can be summarised by its slogan 'No socialism without women's liberation; no women's liberation without socialism.' However even within this statement were contained two dissimilar approaches: one with the goal of extending the role of women in the working-class revolutionary movement, the other with the desire to examine the connection from a position of feminist autonomy. Women involved with this approach to feminism were only too conscious of their inconsistent identity:

We are the daughters of feminism and the labour movement, that is the child of a couple which has always fought and contested each other. And we stagger from one to the other, trying to find our own coherence.[1]

Initially, 'class struggle' feminists tended to see themselves as socialist/revolutionary first and as feminist second. Some of them tried to be both in their mixed political organisation and in the

27

women's movement; others rejected their former organisation because the group's practice systematically ignored women's needs and capacities, but they frequently tried to hold on to the group's political analysis. Contradictions of different kinds emerged. Women who wanted to maintain their 'dual allegiance' found that they were constantly required to justify their continued presence on both fronts. In the MLF, they were immediately suspected of being the spokeswomen of their organisation, and were accused of being sent by men into the MLF in order to spread men's words. They were never totally trusted and were not treated as individual women with individual voices. In the political organisation, the MLF was either ridiculed as hysterical, despised as divisive of the working class, or seen as fresh terrain for recruitment. The substance of the women's feminism was not given any serious political attention within the organisation.

A further contradiction was clear in the way class struggle feminists sometimes tried to remain theoretically faithful to their organisation, while their movement towards feminism in fact made this impossible. The contradiction was evident in their texts. For instance, they were reluctant to name men as oppressors of women and tried hard to avoid it, sometimes going to absurd lengths: 'in spite of your good intentions, you are our oppressors', or 'women are oppressed by the so-called stronger sex'. Men are frequently excused as victims of capitalism. At the more 'workerist' end of the class struggle approach, women refused to attack men on any count, and directed their anger against the bosses. *Femmes travailleuses en lutte* (Women Workers' Struggle), a newspaper put out by women who saw no distinction between women's struggle and the struggle for socialism, stated clearly their position (No. 4, 1975):

We see our struggle as an integral part of the struggle of the working class for socialist revolution. Our struggle against our bosses, against the oppression in our daily lives, against sexism, our taking charge of our own politics, all contribute to the unity of the working class.

When they refer to 'us', they mean the collectivity of women workers together with men workers rather than the collectivity of women. At this end of the class-struggle spectrum also, women seemed unable or unwilling to talk about themselves and their own oppression, and kept their former habit of organising in order to liberate someone other than themselves. They were roundly accused of this in *Le Torchon brûle* (No. 2, 1971) by other women in the MLF, who were discovering the importance of talking about themselves: 'You never say "I", and you always talk about other people, never about yourselves; you talk about the MASSES, whom, as you put it, you want to CONQUER . . .'

Women in this feminist current first organised in local groups and saw their role as a local avant-garde, trying to engage women in conversation at local markets or children's playgrounds and talking to them about their lives and their oppression; their belief in 'entry-ism' made them try to get jobs in factories and firms in order to organise other women employees. They hoped that by hearing the 'Truth', women would join the radical fold. Not surprisingly, this met with relative failure, which in turn led militant women to change their attitudes, look more at their own lives and political beliefs and reassess their approach. The notions of political practice drawn from their political organisations were shown to be ineffective, and the concept of the avant-garde, the enlightened instructing the unen-lightened, was increasingly abandoned and replaced by the process of exchange, self-reflection and support that was being developed inside consciousness-raising groups, and in the MLF generally.

At the other end of the class-struggle feminist spectrum, women found it easier to criticise men and to point out the problems of organised Left political analysis. Many originally class-struggle orientated groups split because some of the women moved away from the organised Left while others remained close to it. The collective of the magazine *Le Temps des femmes* (Women's Time/The Time for Women) is a case in point. One woman explained the split (No. 5, May 1979):

. . . for 'the others' . . . the point was to assert or reassert a 'clear political project'. And because we didn't see this as the point . . . it became impossible to work together . . .

Why shouldn't we be indecisive and uncertain about what we think? There are many of us who, over the last few years, used to think in terms of certainties, of well-defined, clear political and emotional ideas. Just because we've lost them, does it mean that we can't think at all and everything has to stop?

Between these two positions was a gulf that meant that the current as such could not last long: it never found an identity solid enough to sustain it. The case of women who organised within the mainstream parties of the Left will be discussed in a later chapter, but, as Eliane Viennot points out in her article on women and political parties, the problems were always the same:

> The contradiction of belonging both to a movement that insists on its political independence and to an organisation which wants to take over that movement is practically institutionalised and even theorised into a concept of 'dual loyalties' (double bind?) by some women. It is clear that these contradictions can only get worse – and then the only solution is to stop being a feminist. Which is why the great majority of feminists in far Left revolutionary organisations, insisting on remaining feminists and no matter what shape their particular struggle has taken, have only ever found one way to go: out.[2]

Women in the class struggle current had to take sides, make choices about their particular form of radicalism. The question of their relationship to mixed organisations dominated the current's short life and in effect blocked attempts to think and work constructively. By 1976, the current, as such, had disappeared: those women who felt that women's oppression was subordinate to class oppression in the Marxist sense moved away from the un-organised, eclectic MLF and closer to traditional political action; the other women became more politically diverse, identifying first as feminists and becoming absorbed into the rest of the movement.

And yet the question of feminism and the Left still remained acute, and in the late 1970s, women not only formed women's sections inside their political party, but developed a strong feminist critique of their own party. It is clear, then, that although the class struggle current was short-lived and its identity always fragile and vulnerable, the issues – the debate over patriarchy and capitalism, the question of alliances and the autonomy of the MLF, the relation of women to the class structure as defined by Marx – are alive, more widespread through the movement than before, and as seemingly insoluble as they ever were.

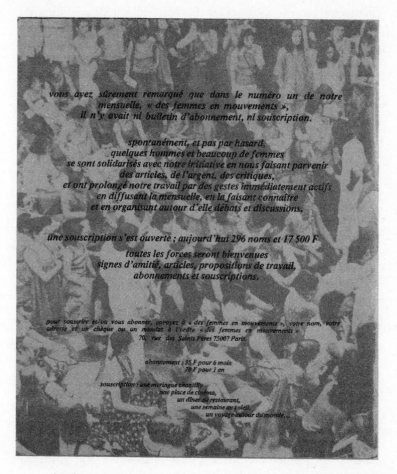

*vous avez sûrement remarqué que dans le numéro un de notre
mensuelle, « des femmes en mouvements »,
il n'y avait ni bulletin d'abonnement, ni souscription.*

*spontanément, et pas par hasard,
quelques hommes et beaucoup de femmes
se sont solidarisés avec notre initiative en nous faisant parvenir
des articles, de l'argent, des critiques,
et ont prolongé notre travail par des gestes immédiatement actifs
en diffusant la mensuelle, en la faisant connaître
et en organisant autour d'elle débats et discussions.*

une souscription s'est ouverte ; aujourd'hui 296 noms et 17 500 F

*toutes les forces seront bienvenues
signes d'amitié, articles, propositions de travail,
abonnements et souscriptions.*

*pour souscrire et/ou vous abonner, envoyez à « des femmes en mouvements », votre nom, votre
adresse et un chèque ou un mandat à l'ordre « des femmes en mouvements »
70, rue des Saints Pères 75007 Paris.*

*abonnement : 35 F pour 6 mois
70 F pour 1 an*

*souscription : une meringue chantilly
une place de cinéma,
un dîner au restaurant,
une semaine au soleil,
un voyage autour du monde...*

des femmes en mouvements, mensuelle, No. 2: inside cover

Psychanalyse et Politique

The group known as *Psych et Po* has had completely different preoccupations from those of women in the class struggle current. While the latter stressed the material conditions of working class women's lives, their exploitation, and oppression under the combined weight of capitalism and patriarchy, *Psych et Po* has consistently emphasised the psychosexual dimension to women's oppression: that is, how 'woman', or 'femininity', is constituted in the first place.

Psych et Po was originally part of a women's study group at the University of Paris at Vincennes. The group described its work in *Le Torchon brûle* (No. 4, 1972) as:

the analysis of our contradictions . . . the work we do using ourselves, our bodies, our unconscious, our sexuality as the starting point, always trying to link subjectivity to history and the political to the sexual.

One woman, psychoanalyst Antoinette Fouque, has been the prime mover of the group, inspiring adoration and loyalty among group participants, who adopted her ideas and her language in much the same way as members of a religious sect follow their leader.

At first, *Psych et Po* was accepted as one group among many, one approach to women's liberation in a movement which valued its diversity and multiplicity of approach. The unlimited funds that seemed to be at the group's disposal benefited all women, as *Psych et Po* were able to found a publishing company, open bookshops and run a magazine (all called *des femmes*). The bookshops were meeting places where women could get information about MLF activities, while the publishing company was an important venture, giving an audience to women's creative expression, which was generally ignored by mainstream publishers.

By the end of the decade, however, actions taken by *Psych et Po* meant that there were two MLFs in France, which would have nothing to do with each other. In 1979, *Psych et Po* registered the name *Mouvement de Libération des Femmes* as their own property, their commercial title, and the logo MLF as their company's trademark. From the group that had favoured underground anonymous activity, *Psych et Po* was transformed into a major business

des femmes en mouvements hebdo No. 44 p. 12

undertaking, involving 3 bookshops, a series of magazines, 3 companies and 4 Associations (which make no profit and are dedicated to research and information).[3] The importance of this for the MLF was that the appropriation of the name could easily mean the appropriation of the whole movement. By owning the name and logo MLF, *Psych et Po* became *the* women's movement instead of part of it; other women are legally barred from speaking as part of the MLF; the media seeks out comments from *Psych et Po* when a feminist comment is wanted, and all in all feminism=MLF=*Psych et Po* operates an unacceptable equation – particularly as *Psych et Po* call themselves anti-feminist. The second decade of the MLF's existence therefore opened with two women's movements in France, one registered, one not, or *marque déposée* and *marque non-déposée*. This schism can never be healed, for it followed at least five years of disputes between *Psych et Po* and various other women's groups over practice, which is the direct result of their analysis.

Psych et Po's analysis has focused on a psychoanalytical approach to the constitution of 'femininity' that is based on the work of psychoanalyst Jacques Lacan. The substance of Lacan's influence on French feminist theory will be more fully discussed in later chapters, but at this point, it should be noted that *Psych et Po* accept Lacan's interpretation of how the child becomes a social subject. For Lacan, the resolution of the Oedipus complex marks the child's acquisition of language and simultaneously his/her entry into the Symbolic. That is, through the resolution of the Oedipus complex, the child (hopefully) rejects the mother's body, identifies with the father in whom the authority of society resides (and is accepted by the mother) and begins to function as a social subject. The child does not merely use language, but is constructed by language at the same time: language is not simply the medium for social interaction, but structures the way that thought itself is formulated, organised and expressed. It is the way that the patriarchal organisation of society enters into the unconscious and, if we are to function adequately in society, absorbs us all into it.

For *Psych et Po*, as for certain other feminist theorists, this process of structuring the social subject suppresses or represses the feminine element in all of us. *Psych et Po* claim that there are, at the outset, two kinds of libidinal economy (organisation of life forces, energy): the masculine and the feminine, from which all behaviour and attributes are derived. In their understanding of sexuality, the feminine libidinal economy has never been allowed to express itself. For *Psych et Po*, little girls have a totally different relationship to the mother, to their own bodies, that can never find expression because society's law is patriarchal, masculine, and forces girls into a society that cannot permit of, nor account for, their difference: language cannot express it, male sexuality distorts female sexuality and the structures in which we think cannot grasp the feminine except as the negative pole of the masculine/feminine opposition. *Psych et Po* say that women as women, that is, as possessing an unrepressed feminine libidinal economy, have never existed: women have been absorbed into a masculine, misogynistic world, have unconsciously internalised masculinity and do not yet know what women could be, what their true selves might be.

Psych et Po's work, their mission, is to make this existence possible, to bring the feminine into existence, and they have tried to develop a number of strategies aiming to defy and undermine masculinity. These strategies operate at different levels. First, in group meetings and in individual analysis (frequently on Antoinette Fouque's couch), each woman must try to understand how she has been made a misogynist – how the masculine elements in her head work against her – and work towards total elimination of these elements, freedom from any dependence on men and on male thinking. Only when women have fully understood their own misogyny, can they work on, learn to develop, and appreciate, their femininity.

The feminine element in us, radically other, can only be developed in autonomous female spaces; hence the founding of the publishing company, the bookshops, the group meetings, the magazine. *Psych et Po* provide physical and textual female spaces in which the feminine can emerge and grow. They emphasise writing as a practice that defies the Logos – the male (Father's) spoken word – and encourage a strategy of writing that undermines the function of language as a tool for the naming and ordering of experience by masculinity, using words in such a way as to bring out many possibilities for meanings, disobeying the rules of structure and syntax. *Psych et Po* also emphasise what they call 'erotic independence', that is, women's homosexual practice, not as a political choice of the kind meant by radical lesbians, but as resistance to 'Oedipisation' through a return to intimacy with the mother's body.

Psych et Po's goal was to be at the forefront of the 'Revolution of the Symbolic', their desire was radically to upset the entire conceptual framework in which we think and act, so that the feminine can be inserted into a totally new relation between masculinity and femininity. A first stage of attacking the way that patriarchy acts upon us is to reverse the hierarchy of values common to our thinking, rejecting all characteristics qualified as masculine, and praising all that is supposedly feminine. For instance, *Psych et Po* describe masculine and feminine power (in *Le Torchon brûle* No. 3, 1972) as follows:

Women's power isn't legal, patriarchal, sadistic, pederastic, it isn't concerned with representation, with leadership, with names, with rape, repression, hatred, avarice, knowledge, order, individualism, with abstractions.

It's a non-power of the matrix, of birthings, givings, chaos, differences, of collective freedoms, of openings, of bodies, of recognitions, of lifting censorships, of pleasure, outside the law, it's a power-to, act-think-do, by/for all women, all.

This enormous enterprise seems to involve the construction of an autonomous women's Utopia; their attempt to think women's autonomy in non-patriarchal terms seems to mean placing themselves outside patriarchy. 'We are elsewhere' reads one of their tracts; their publishing project is described as 'going beyond the present historical moment'. Through understanding masculinity and femininity, *Psych et Po* claim to have vanquished oppression and are now unreachable: 'our space, impregnable.' *Psych et Po*, assimilating themselves with the feminine, do not simply take on single-handed the battle against masculinity, but have already won: in bringing the feminine into existence, they seem to think that they are the first 'real' women.

Psych et Po present a global analysis in the light of which the women involved can engage in a particular kind of struggle for a particular kind of women's liberation: everything can be explained in terms of women's radical alterity, difference. The group's actions derive closely from their analysis, indeed the group's emphasis on theory was itself never the problem: what became the problem was the consequence of the crusade for recovery of the feminine in practical, tangible terms for the MLF.

In a sense, the registration of the name and logo of the women's movement was a logical conclusion to an analysis that insists that it is the only real challenge to patriarchy and does not accept the validity of any other. They could be seen as saving the MLF from 'feminism', that is, from what they define as feminism which encompasses all politically active, non-*Psych et Po* women from the sister of the Shah of Iran to Simone de Beauvoir, from conservative women politicians to anarchists. For *Psych et Po*, feminists merely want to replace men in seats of power without really changing anything.

The goal of being the only women's liberation movement in France is also evident in their magazine, *des femmes en mouvements* (women in movement/women on the move) which appeared at first on a monthly and then a weekly basis. A careful reading of the magazine leaves a strange aftertaste. The tone of the writing is consistently self-congratulatory. All MLF initiatives are claimed as their own; themes are always treated from the perspective of feminine difference; issues which cannot fit into their scheme of things are avoided; the same concepts and vocabulary are used time and time again. *Psych et Po* groups all over France are praised for bringing women to the light; letters are published, apparently from women the world over, of the 'I was lost and now I'm found' kind, thanking *Psych et Po*. In *la Revue d'en face* (No.8, p.37, 1980) radical feminist Marie-Jo Dhavernas has pointed out the repetitive style of the articles and letters, which, together with the anonymity of the authors, makes her suspicious: 'it is *des femmes*/women/some women, who are speaking, and I'll bet you that when you compare two articles, you can't tell whether or not they have been written by the same person.'

The magazines are glossy, well-presented. The group clearly does not suffer from the same financial straits as most feminist groups. The magazines are scattered with photographs of women together, smiling, in beautiful natural settings. All is harmony in the image of the women's movement that they propose. Women are creative together, they dance, sing and struggle together (always successfully) in the warm complicity of sisterhood. Oppression has been overcome, pain is gone. Liliane Kandel, a feminist who has exposed *Psych et Po's* co-option strategy and has analysed their journals, expressed the unease felt by many women when faced with this image of the women's movement, when she wrote (*Questions féministes* No. 7, p. 34, 1980):

What about women who have doubts? Women who are suffering? Or are in despair? Or dying? There is no room for them in this scenario, unchanging and unchangeable, where the

LE MOUVEMENT DE LIBERATION DES FEMMES RESTERA-T-IL LA PROPRIETE PRIVEE D'UN GROUPE ?

Si Psych & Po est le MLF
Je ne suis pas au MLF
Or, je suis au Mouvement de Libération des Femmes
Donc, Psych & Po n'est pas le Mouvement de Libération des Femmes
(ni le MLF)

Depuis dix ans, des femmes se réunissent entre elles de façon indépendante et non mixte pour lutter contre l'oppression patriarcale sous toutes ses formes. Ces groupes n'ont jamais voulu constituer un parti ni même une organisation, et ne le veulent toujours pas. C'est l'ensemble de ces groupes et individues qui s'est nommé : Mouvement de Libération des Femmes, et que les media ont appelé « MLF ». C'est pourquoi aucun groupe ne s'est jamais donné le droit de s'appeler *Mouvement de Libération des Femmes* à lui seul, respectant ainsi la diversité théorique et pratique de l'ensemble du Mouvement.

Or aujourd'hui un de ces groupes — qui utilise indifféremment les signatures suivantes : « Psychanalyse et Politique », « Des femmes en mouvements » (mensuelle et hebdo), Sarl Editions et Librairie « Des Femmes », « Des femmes du MLF » — revendique la propriété exclusive du Mouvement de Libération des Femmes.
Ce groupe, « Psychanalyse et Politique », vient de se constituer en association régie par la loi de 1901, avec pouvoir juridique, sous le nom : *Mouvement de Libération des Femmes (MLF)* (cf. le Journal Officiel du 30 octobre 1979, p.8817).

Ce dépôt est scandaleux en ce qu'il dépossède toutes les femmes de ce qui définit leur démarche politique; par lui, une seule tendance du Mouvement s'approprie l'histoire et les luttes collectives des femmes. En outre, de nombreux groupes et individues du Mouvement de Libération des Femmes se situent plutôt hors les lois que dans la loi; elles n'admettent pas que « Des Femmes » (marque déposée) les y inscrive. Par cette mainmise, le terme « Mouvement de Libération des Femmes (MLF) » désigne maintenant juridiquement un seul groupe (qui se déclare ouvertement « anti-féministe »...) et une seule pratique, dans lesquels nous ne nous reconnaissons pas et que nous ne voulons pas avoir à assumer.

En tant que femmes du Mouvement de Libération des Femmes, nous disons :

Il n'est pas question qu'elles conservent abusivement ce titre

Courrier à *FMA* * - BP 370 - 75625 PARIS Cedex 13

* Cette boîte postale a déjà servi à un grand nombre d'actions et initiatives du Mouvement de Libération des Femmes, en particulier : le Manifeste des 343, le Torchon brûle, les journées de dénonciation des crimes contre les femmes (Paris, Mai 72), la Marche Nationale des femmes (6 octobre 79).

NOM   ADRESSE   SIGNATURE

Signataires (au 19 décembre 1979) :

Collectif de la Marche du 6 octobre; Ligue du Droit des Femmes; Les Répondeuses; le centre Flora Tristan pour femmes battues (Clichy); *Histoires d'Elles*; SOS-Femme Alternative; *La Revue d'En Face (moins une)*; Les Babouches; Le Temps des Femmes; *Questions féministes*; FMA; Le centre de documentation féministe; Les derniers dinosaures avant l'autoroute; le Collectif féministe contre la répression; CIDF; *Elles voient rouge*; MLAC; Collectif de la Maison des femmes (rue Saint-Sabin, Paris); A tire d'elles; le Collectif « Paroles »; Les femmes s'en mêlent.

35

Petition aginst the appropriation of the name MLF

struggle is always glorious, always righteous and always invincible, with Great Feminine Leaps Forward.

Kandel's fear was that *Psych et Po's* copyrighting the name MLF would give public sanction to their view of women's oppression and liberation, and reduce other groups to impotent opposition or to silence. The desire legally to fuse together *Psych et Po – des femmes* with *des femmes* (women), making themselves the legal, recognised representatives of women's resistance to patriarchy, was ruthless in that it prevented all other women from using the logo MLF, or from calling themselves part of the women's liberation movement in France: by 'squatting' the name, *Psych et Po* kept everyone else.

Some feminists responded by shrugging their shoulders and deciding to carry on as usual, but others, including Kandel, have seen the copyrighting as a dangerous political strategy 'the monopoly of the women's liberation movement – either to capture it or to destroy it'. A major campaign was mounted against *Psych et Po* to expose its actions and thereby destroy its credibility. The group has never felt the need to respond to this massive opposition and never deals with political opposition from feminists. Opposition is explained away in psychoanalytic terms, turned into expressions of hate or fear, dismissed as hysterical, when the group responds at all.

The decade of the 1970s closed with much feminist energy directed at publicly discrediting *Psych et Po*, who were able to appear aloof and aggrieved. However, with the election of the Socialists to power and the setting up of the Ministry for Women's Rights, *Psych et Po* have taken a back seat. Their co-option strategy seems to have failed; they have not benefited from the change of government; they have not silenced other women; they have not taken over the MLF's life. In 1984, no-one in the MLF (*marque non-déposée*) seems to give *Psych et Po* much thought; new problems seem far more pressing. Antoinette Fouque has gone to live in the United States, where *Psych et Po* has aroused a lot of interest, and she returns from time to time to run her companies; the magazine has ceased publication; the bookshops and publishing company are attempting to be commercial enterprises rather than political ventures, and the group presents no threat.

Non-aligned feminism

The third current to be discussed here was born out of the group *Féministes Révolutionnaires*, who had been responsible for the 'spectacular' actions that brought the MLF into the public arena. Its identity is hard to trace except by defining it in relation to what it isn't: that is, it consists of those women and groups who do not subscribe to a doctrine that fits women's oppression into the framework of a ready-made theory, be it Marxist, Maoist or Lacanian. The women forming these non-aligned feminist groups work around specific projects rather than around a specific global analysis. This feminism, probably the most familiar to women in other countries, and certainly the kind with which I feel most comfortable, lives in small collectives, individual research and collective actions, attempting to get by from day to day and to work out any theoretical positions from daily experience, grounded in the reality of women's lives. Not cemented together by any collectively held belief in either the imminence of the revolution or the advent of the feminine, these non-aligned groups have been particularly susceptible to splits in the collectives, as both individuals and groups evolve; new mobilising issues have to be sought, and after each event or campaign, they have to reassess and rethink positions, as no consistent outlook sustains them.

Non-aligned feminism must, precisely because of its non-alignment, be understood in its plurality, committed as the women are to a multiplicity of voices and actions, to dialogue and openness. Non-aligned feminists differ significantly from the class struggle current women in that they rejected known political organisations, policies and practices from the beginning, and have therefore not been plagued by the confusions and difficulties of contradictory allegiance seen in class struggle current feminists. They also differ from *Psych et Po* women in that they remained suspicious of all theory that claims to explain everything in global terms, and they rejected the uniformity that *Psych et Po* seemed to require and the hierarchical grouping around Antoinette.

The goals of non-aligned feminism have always been diverse. At the beginning, the *Féministes Révolutionnaires* said (*Le Torchon brûle* No.5, 1973) that they wanted to 'encourage all women to take charge of their own lives, think for themselves, take initiatives, be creative, while refusing to integrate into the society we live in'. By feminist, they meant 'Above all, for women and with all women', and by revolutionary, they meant 'we don't want to improve the conditions of our detention, we want to turn the whole place upside-down.' This rather broad definition was further widened by women in the *Féministes Révolutionnaires* deciding to work on a wide variety of projects, some of which were called 'reformist', and others which helped to constitute a network of alternative support for women. Projects proliferated, from study groups in universities to women's cafés and feminist newspapers.

I would not like to suggest, however, that non-aligned feminists are unconcerned with formulating analyses of women's oppression. Some collectives are deeply engaged in this. For instance, the women who produced the journal *Questions féministes* stated in their first issue that their goal was to build a theory of women's oppression based on the premise that women form a social class of gender and are oppressed by the social class of men. To eliminate this oppression, its social roots must be exposed, explained, attacked and dismantled. Notions that support the existence of essential differences between men and women that go beyond the biological, that suggest the possibility of something outside the social, are rejected: women and men are made, not born. In their first editorial (1977) the *Questions féministes* collective said clearly the opposite of *Psych et Po*:

> We believe that there is no such thing as a direct relationship to the body; to say that there is, is not subversive, because it denies the existence and the power of social forces – the very forces that oppress us, oppress our bodies.

Questions féministes rejects any attempt to 'think, construct, propose any idea of Woman outside society'. Their ideal would be eventually for women to be able to say: 'I will not be a woman or a man in the way we understand the words today; I will be a Person in a woman's body.' Members of the *Questions Féministes* collective are concerned to examine patriarchy as a system, studying aspects of it such as domestic labour, women in the family, the status of agricultural wives, as well as focusing on patriarchal ideology. Most recently those members of the original collective who are now producing *Nouvelles Questions féministes*, have put out a special issue on

Histoires d'elles Nos. 1 and 2

women and the state, made especially pertinent by the change of government.

Questions féministes was generally felt to represent the hard line of radical feminism that is only one part of non-aligned feminism. Other collectives, other journals, have tried to fulfil a variety of functions that mix militancy and theory. For instance *Histoires d'elles* wanted to cover a whole range of issues, bring feminist viewpoints to bear on world events and reflect on them through the prism of women's experience of them, as well as discuss the development of feminist theory and also reflect the life of the MLF. *Histoires d'elles* had a vision of their project that was open, supportive of differences (No.6, p.15, 1977):

we want it (the paper) to show up our contradictions, reflect the difficulties that run through the women's movement, we don't want to pretend that we have the answers, we don't see women as a myth of redemption, but as our reality, full of contradictions.

Because of its wide range of involvements, and its absence of one clear conceptual framework, non-aligned feminism can be characterised by the combination of registers present in their texts, the different modes of expression and the juxtaposition of styles that accommodate the diverse aspects of their explorations and reflect individual personalities and collective preoccupations. There is movement between the personal and the theoretical, the pragmatic and the analytical, the descriptive and the prescriptive. As *Histoires d'elles* said of their own project (No.19, p, 2, 1980):

On principle we wouldn't set up a fixed collective political line . . . it is precisely diversity and contradiction that seem to be elements of richness, of life, of openness . . . and again, we won't try to fuse different voices in a way that would make us representatives of all women and would also hide our own identity behind what others are saying.

Non-aligned feminism can equally be characterised by its positive aspects, not simply by what it rejects. Positive principles were adopted for the working out of new theory and practice, which were born of the rejection of existent political discourse and practices. There was first the firmly held belief that 'the personal is political' and second, there was the insistence on rigorous equality, rejection of leadership and women speaking for themselves and for themselves only.

The expression 'the personal is political' may be overused and hackneyed, but it has very concrete meanings. Above all, it means that politics is about personal life, not simply about electoral battles and ambitious individuals: that the way we live in our private lives is as much the stuff of politics as parliamentary debates or theories of the state; and that 'the political' shapes our lives beyond that which is generally recognised. The result is a redefinition of politics which destroys the barriers between public and private life and therefore opens up questions about what can and cannot be discussed in political terms. Left-wing male political activists had too frequently not modified their private lives to synchronise with their liberating speeches, neglecting to apply their principles for the future to their own lives in the present. For feminists, any programme for liberation had to include the substance of our everyday lives, and issues such as childcare and housework can no longer be dismissed as trivial – as 'women's stuff'. This insistence on the interpenetration of the personal and the political is at the base of all non-aligned feminist thinking, with women's experience considered to be the testing ground for the validity of any theory.

'The personal is political' also had far-reaching implications for the language in which 'politics' is discussed. Traditional political terminology was felt to be too formal, too abstract and removed from women's reality. To reassess the political meant to write differently, to speak differently. The early years of the MLF saw the telling of personal life stories, self-revelation, anecdotes and grievances as the way to ensure the link between the person and politics. Women talking about themselves created a different relation to their own words, meant a high degree of personal implication and vulnerability, and changed the way that women both used, and listened to, language. Listening was re-evaluated and women's words given the attention and seriousness due them: women remembered the self-consciousness and humiliation of being ignored and ridiculed as so many had felt in their mixed political groups, and tried to avoid this silencing of other women. This intimidation that women had experienced led to the adoption of the principle of segregation for meetings. While the women-only nature of feminism has not abolished power play in feminist groups, it has meant that certain problems have been avoided. As Dale Spender quotes in *Man-Made Language*, when men were not present, 'there was no need to argue about whether the problems we felt were real.'[4] When men are not present, women talk in different ways – there is a complicity between women that forms the basis of women's solidarity, and that is instantly lost when men are there. Examining this language of complicity, giving a political dimension to 'chatting', 'gossiping', is an essential part of the attempt to abolish the distance between political discourse and women's lives, an understanding about how language plays upon us and the need to modify it.

The second principle, or guideline, for non-aligned feminists, was the insistence on equality and the emphasis on collective work. Women refused to place their faith in a leader, in a party, in a text, which would take responsibility for them and tell them what to do. Collective elaboration of ideas was intended to foster a sense of solidarity, to encourage exchange of ideas, avoid power relations inside groups and encourage a sense of both personal and collective identity. Equality is one thing in theory but another in practice as women soon realised. One New York consciousness-raising group instituted a system of tokens to ensure equal participation in group meetings. At the beginning of each meeting, each woman had the same number of small tokens, and each time she spoke, she used up a token. This had the comical result that, on one occasion, all the tokens were used up in the first ten minutes, and on another, all the tokens were so jealously guarded that nobody spoke at all.[5]

There were also more insidious problems connected with the question of leadership that applied to French feminists as to others. As Jo Freeman pointed out in the early 1970s, rejection of explicit leadership by no means meant absence of implicit leadership: in every group, there is a complicated network of relationships, with in-groups and outsiders, personal preferences, stronger and less influential voices. Marie-Jo Dhavernas put it more cynically when she said (*la Revue d'en Face* No. 11, p. 33, 1981) 'Show me your address book and I'll tell you who you are in the women's movement.' Absence of formal leadership was intended to allow each woman to participate fully in decision-making and have an equal influence in the group. Its actual effect was to generate endless discussion before any decision could be reached, and it encouraged the arguments that have plagued the MLF. Because there were no agreed organisational principles, there was no generally acceptable or accepted way of quelling dissatisfaction, and all collectives, of whatever nature, have been subject to rifts and splits.

This question of leadership and structure has haunted non-aligned feminist groups and has proved to be its greatest internal problem. It is paradoxical that the greatest strength of non-aligned feminism – lack of dogmatism, openness and plurality of approach, belief in the value of each woman's contribution – is also its weakness. Non-aligned feminist insistence on refusal of structure, believing that to adopt a fixed structure would be to destroy the dynamism of the MLF, means that when organisation is needed, it is carried out by ad hoc committees which are dissolved once the action or event has taken place. There is no continuity of action, no overall strategy to provide a framework for action, no grand scheme for justifying them. The lack of a coherent revolutionary project partly explains the way that many militant feminists feel ineffective and frustrated and abandon their militancy; it means that it is capable of change and is more adaptable than other types of feminism, but its identity has to be constantly reinforced and reasserted; it means that while it is more open and permeable to what is going on around it, it is also more vulnerable to pressures from outside and to fluctuations in the political climate.

These three approaches clearly have certain elements in common and others that divide them irrevocably. The principal factor dividing groups lies in the overall approach: whether their feminism excludes others and is determined according to a set of principles defined once and for all, or whether it is still trying to formulate the questions rather than provide the answers. This opposition of approach in fact cuts across the groups to a certain extent. The tension within class struggle current feminism was precisely due to the existence of both an exclusive and an open approach within what was trying to be one current; and within non-aligned feminism, radical feminism is more clear about its premises than other feminist groups.[6] As groups of women identify their aims and ideas, some will split away from the main body of the MLF; or as one issue causes intense conflict, it will provoke a split. This primary tension is created by the very multiplicity of the MLF: the two conflicting approaches – the closed, coherent worldview versus the open experiential practice – cannot find a middle point of reconciliation. Built into each approach is an element that rejects the other and makes compromise impossible.

To illustrate the implications of this conflictual internal dynamic, and to discuss the evolution of MLF arguments in a more specific way, I will turn to look at one area of significant feminist debate and action: in exploring how feminists in France have approached the question of motherhood through the decade of the 1970s, my general arguments about the MLF will be anchored in a more concrete way, and located in the context of the issue that was the first, most widely mobilising campaign of the MLF.

LE TORCHON BRULE

LIBERATION DES FEMMES

n? 4

Menstruel 1F

CHAPTER 3

French feminists and motherhood: destiny or slavery?

I have chosen to focus on motherhood for this illustrative chapter for several reasons. As it is at the heart of women's 'condition', it is central to feminist analysis; as a question that raises attitudes that defy logic and reason, it affects women on different levels and resists attempts to apply a simple political solution to its problems; as the first concerted campaign by feminists in France, the fight for voluntary maternity was a hugely successful but equally problem-laden mobilising issue, which highlights the different political positions and preoccupations of different feminist approaches, and shows the way in which the various groups, and the MLF as a whole, evolved over the decade.

In 1970, the family was analysed as the cause of women's specific oppression, and feminists almost universally agreed that motherhood, defining and limiting women, had to be rejected in capitalist society. During the course of the decade, this rejection was gradually seen as oversimplifying the issue, and a search for ways of making motherhood more acceptable began: a search for ways to retain womanhood and individual identity in motherhood. In the latter part of the 1970s, an attempt was therefore begun to find a third way of thinking about motherhood that conformed to neither of the two caricatural poles which conceived of motherhood as either destiny or slavery. These two images reflect the two extremes of feminist analysis in France: concentration on the ideological oppression that forces women into motherhood or on the bodily experiences of maternity as an experience specific to women and therefore to be prized. The different dimensions of motherhood – the socio-political,

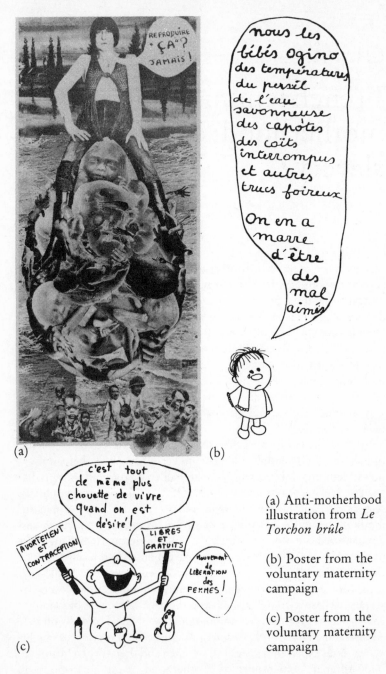

(a) Anti-motherhood illustration from *Le Torchon brûle*

(b) Poster from the voluntary maternity campaign

(c) Poster from the voluntary maternity campaign

the psycho-sexual and the symbolic – have never been appre-hended in their unity. They may overlap in feminist discussions, but one aspect or another is always given a privileged position in relation to the others, showing the priorities of the different approaches and highlighting the winding paths taken by the MLF over the decade of the 1970s. In reading the texts – books, articles, poetry, letters and stories in the feminist press – a clear pattern emerges. From heavy concentration on abortion-law reform in the early part of the 1970s, feminists went on to consider the difficult and contradictory feelings raised by the actual experiences of pregnancy and childbirth, the confusions about choice that availability of contraception and abortion meant. By the end of the decade, the image of woman-as-mother, rejected in the beginning, was being reassessed rather than rejected.

From 1970 to 1975, the analysis of motherhood was almost exclusively tied to the campaign for free, legal abortion on demand, and the diffusion of information about, and free availability to all women of contraception. This fight was an issue that all feminists agreed on, holding the same basic premise, 'the right to control our own bodies'. Interpretations of this varied, and the tactics employed in the struggle were disputed, but this issue caused no violent splits in the MLF, nor disagreements that impeded action.

Some pro-abortion arguments were aired before the existence of the MLF, from a different perspective. Some argued that the 1920 law – which operated against the abortioner, the woman aborting and all those who helped her procure an abortion – was impossible to put into practice and lagged behind public mores. Others believed that selective 'therapeutic' abortion would provide a practical solution to certain problem pregnancies. The MLF approach broke with this totally, and was the first to treat contraception and abortion as part of the same issue, namely, women's right to control their own bodies.

In the first MLF texts to deal with abortion and contraception, the emphasis was heavily on class. In examining the 1920 law, the women who wrote *Matières pour une réflexion politique sur l'avortement* – (Towards a Political Analysis of Abortion),[1] concluded that the law was aimed against the working class, as bourgeois women had access to contraception and to private abortions in clinics, in conditions of discretion and safety. They saw the function of the abortion law as keeping intact the status quo of capitalist society, which could not allow women to question their role as mothers because it would destroy the ideology of the family, which in turn is the mainstay of capitalism. This article suggests that capitalism would collapse if women withheld their reproductive power: 'ideologically and economically, society cannot allow women to refuse to have babies: so it does everything it can to repress any questioning, any rejection, of motherhood.' The logical way to undermine the foundations of capitalism would be for women to reappropriate their reproductive power and refuse to have children for the capitalist state: motherhood would only be acceptable for women after the socialist revolution.

These early class struggle current inspired texts treated motherhood as purely negative and claimed that this was the only possible light in which to see it. The illegality of abortion and the difficulty of obtaining contraception meant that motherhood was not a woman's choice about her own life, but was outside her own control. The main need expressed by these articles on abortion was to show that women shared a certain condition that was a political condition demanding a political solution, and not the 'natural' and the only role for women.

One text that showed that abortion was a question for all women, regardless of class position, and that brought the issue of the reform of the abortion law to the centre of the public's attention, was the Manifesto in *Le Nouvel Observateur* quoted in Chapter 1. The 343 well-known women who signed the Manifesto and declared publicly that they had aborted made it possible for the first time to admit that one had had an abortion, a fact that had previously been a secret kept out of shame and fear. Many of the women who signed the Manifesto had not actually aborted, which was significant in that, as Danièle Léger noted, 'by signing, they recognised that the need for an abortion concentrated in an extreme way all the various aspects of the specific oppression of women.'[2] Women's social and sexual submission, and economic and emotional dependance on men are encapsulated in the question of abortion – the pressures to conform to the social norm of motherhood within marriage, the concept of conjugal rights, the illegality (until 1967) of contraception and of abortion (until 1975), all added up to a situation for women where their bodies were controlled by others. It was this understanding of the wider significance of the abortion law that made the fight for free legal abortion on demand so fundamental a part of the feminist struggle. The publication of the Manifesto marked the point following which the issue of abortion and contraception was situated in the global context of women's liberation as an essential right of all women, no longer to be considered as an unfortunate and unmentionable practical solution to individual problems.

The Manifesto also marked the beginning of an intensive campaign for the abolition of the abortion law in which not only women of the MLF were involved. As well as the MLF, there was the MLAC, *Choisir* and the *Groupe Information Santé* – GIS (Health Information Group). The relationship of the MLF to these other organisations, all concerned for their own reasons with the abortion campaign, was never smooth and showed up those problems that would go on to divide the women in the MLF amongst themselves. *Choisir* had precise and limited goals when it was founded, and wanted to concentrate on abortion law reform without placing it in the context of women's liberation; the GIS, composed of doctors who wanted to change the nature of medical practice, saw the issue of abortion in terms of what was wrong with medicine rather than in terms of women; and the MLAC considered that their open, illegal practice of abortion was part of their revolutionary practice, and to a large extent, saw the abortion campaign as a good mobilising issue.

The MLAC, the GIS and *Choisir*, as well as class struggle current feminists, placed abortion and contraception in the context of class, rather than as an issue concerning all women. They felt that bourgeois women with money to pay for private doctors were not affected by the law, and that their evasion of the law was tolerated, while working-class women paid the penalty of poverty. This approach was highlighted in 1972 at the trial in the Paris suburb of Bobigny of four women who had helped the daughter of one of them, Marie-Claire Chevalier, procure an abortion. The lawyers, with Maître Gisele Halimi at their head, successfully defended the women (who were found guilty but whose nominal fine of 8 francs really indicated victory) and turned the trial into a test case against the 1920 law. An array of celebrities, guaranteed to impress the French public and the courts, testified on scientific, humanitarian and feminist grounds.[3] The case was fought on the premise that the law hit working-class women, and the lawyers focused on the conditions of illegal abortions, not on abortion itself as a fundamental right. As Maître Halimi said in her summing up:

It is always the same class that suffers: the class of poor women, economically and socially vulnerable, the class with no money and no contacts.[4]

Apart from women with a class struggle orientation to feminism, the MLF contested this class bias, and based their own attack on the law on the simple fact that abortion/pregnancy is a woman's body, a woman's life and therefore a woman's choice. Halimi felt that the approach proposed by the MLF would have alienated sympathy for the cause rather than attract it. The MLF apparently wanted to conduct the defence by calling a series of witnesses, all women, none famous, to say that they had aborted and felt well and happy. Although understanding the motives behind this, Halimi thought that this approach was guaranteed to alienate the public and would serve neither the interests of women generally nor those of the Chevaliers in particular. She wrote later that:

> I wanted to . . . denounce the hypocrisy of the law, show up religious and social taboos, received wisdoms and official reasons like the low birth rate, respect for life, etc. for what they are . . . and reveal the drama of backstreet abortion and the repressive nature of class justice in an unbearable, blinding light.[5]

However, by placing abortion in the context of a general, non-feminist revolutionary practice as did the MLAC, or by using it as a single issue campaign divorced from feminist practice as did *Choisir*, by reintroducing men into the struggle and by fighting the abortion law using class-based arguments, the original feminist premise was lost. Women's own voices were absent from MLAC texts in which the question of abortion no longer seemed to be connected to women's reality. The MLF and the MLAC parted company. The MLF also rejected *Choisir* on several grounds: it was claimed that Halimi was using women to further her own career; the MLF objected to the parade of celebrities at Bobigny and to the way that *Choisir* seemed to court respectability.

Most of all, in the Bobigny trial, the MLF objected to the way that abortion was abstracted from any analysis of women's specific oppression. A non-aligned feminist approach to abortion and contraception considers motherhood, voluntary motherhood, to be an issue that is a women's issue, to do with women's bodies and lives regardless of class and regardless of revolutionary practice:

> let society make eggs, fertilise them, throw up in the mornings, let
> society get huge, so huge that it can't get through the metro
> turnstiles, let society have backache and let it give birth. As long
> as it does none of these things, society can't tell us what to do.[6]

The anger in this quotation, the insistence on women's own experience, shows rage at the fact that this abstraction 'society' has the right
to decide the fate of women without paying the slightest attention to
the lived dimension of an unwanted pregnancy, which for many
feminists was a potent symbol of women's oppression.

The different emphasis – on class oppression or on women's
oppression – affected every aspect of feminist analysis in the first few
years, with loyalties uncompromisingly divided. As far as voluntary
maternity was concerned, it meant that while all groups wanted the
abolition of the 1920 law, no agreement could be reached over how to
obtain their demands nor about the terms in which to frame their
arguments. While mixed organisations and reform-minded organisations believed that the law should allow women to choose their
pregnancies, class struggle current feminists insisted that motherhood had to be rejected in capitalist society, for under capitalism
there was no such thing as free choice, and this perspective dominated
the MLF for the first two years of the campaign.

After that, the MLF began to develop its own autonomous analyses of the voluntary maternity issue. Two of these are particularly
interesting: a collectively-written book called *Maternité esclave* (Enslaved Motherhood) and a pamphlet called *Libérer nos corps ou
libérer l'avortement?* (Liberate our Bodies or Liberate Abortion?).

Maternité esclave[7] was written by a specially formed collective
who were part of the *Féministes Révolutionnaires*. Its general theme
is well-expressed in the title, but, as well as developing the theme of
motherhood as slavery in capitalist society, the book has a second
aim: to provide practical information about the processes that lead to
pregnancy for women for whom basic information about menstrua-
tion, conception and childbirth was often difficult to find. These two
goals do not fit well together. The authors' clear attitude that
motherhood means slavery designed to keep women subordinate and
dependent on men, does not permit a positive appraisal of what is
physiologically and emotionally involved for women who insist on
enslaving themselves. The practical side of the book is therefore

55

extremely curt – for instance, the sum of the book's comment on pregnancy is 'embryonic life begins. It will last nine months'.

Motherhood itself, divorced from the current social setting is not attacked:

> the only logical choice for us is to reject motherhood as long as procreation and childcare are considered as one and the same thing. What makes motherhood unbearable are the conditions imposed on mothers in our society, obviously not motherhood in and of itself.

The authors have clear ideas about the meaning of the abortion campaign, which is part of a long-term vision of disrupting the institutions of marriage and the family, and must not be abstracted from this goal:

> The only point of fighting for abortion and contraception is if it is used to shake up and in the long term destroy marriage and the family, which maintain women's and children's slavery, and constitute the foundations of . . . authoritarian social systems.

Like other early feminist texts, then, *Maternité esclave* considered that motherhood could only ever be acceptable once it no longer meant slavery, which in turn meant overturning all the pressures – legal, psychological, economic – which make motherhood within marriage the only viable social model for adult women to conform to, and give to mothers the sole real charge of their children's welfare. Most of the book therefore concentrates on ways to avoid motherhood, and the rest of it explains exactly why motherhood is slavery, showing its costs in terms of women's lives and women's bodies. The authors believed that a political analysis of motherhood revealed that the capitalist state needed women at home, providing free domestic labour and creating the workforce of the future: like the women who wrote *Matières* . . ., these authors felt that rejection of motherhood was a demonstration of women's power and ability to undermine capitalism. Furthermore, acceptance of the role of mother was simply falling into a patriarchal trap.

Libérer nos corps ou libérer l'avortement? was first published in 1972 in *Le Torchon brûle* – No. 5, called *Avortement, contraception, sexualité, réformisme* and written by women in the *Féministes*

Révolutionnaires group – and was later re-named and reprinted by *des femmes*. In this pamphlet, abortion and contraception as an issue is located in the context of women's sexuality in a critique of heterosexual relations, analysed as male domination of women in an institutionalised, oppressive power structure. 'Abortion is aggression and power over our bodies. It is a reminder of a sexuality that is predicated on aggression and on the exploitation of women's bodies'. The heart of the text is the search for a different light in which to define women's sexuality, and the authors suggest that the dominant way of thinking about abortion and contraception either obscures or avoids the roots of what it is really at stake:

No-one has raised the question of the relationship of the body to the unconscious, and so the problem of women's relationship to a body that she doesn't control, a body denied and censored by the system, is hidden.

They argue that heterosexuality, based on the denial of women's sexuality, is inherently violent – an analysis which would logically lead to an outright rejection of heterosexuality itself. However, this is not the conclusion that is reached, except implicitly, in the text. The conclusion confronts the dilemma that women find themselves in where reproduction is concerned. On the one hand, it is reproductive power, production of life, that separates women from men and marks women's difference, but on the other, this same capacity locks women into oppressive power structures. The authors do not see contraception as an answer: 'It would mean that we want to be like men; it means refusing ovulation, the functioning of the matrix . . . which is the only thing that allows us to identify ourselves, identify ourselves as women.' But motherhood doesn't provide an answer either: '(we must) . . . reject the power structure that oppresses us even in our relations to those around us and in our sexual lives; we must refuse to ally the satisfaction of our needs and desires to the production needs of capitalism.'

The authors seem to agree with the analysis dominant in the early 1970s, that is, that motherhood as a positive experience must wait until after the collapse of capitalism. But the authors go further than other feminists at that time and suggest that, in fact, the only truly satisfactory method of contraception is psychically produced, either psychically provoked abortion, or psychically provoked blockage of ovulation. This 'method' avoids the use of any techniques, avoids male power over women by retaining fertility (women's power) but rejecting fertilisation (men's power).

This conclusion is curious unless it is read as showing that there is simply no satisfactory answer to unwanted pregnancy, and that women need control over what happens to their bodies. But the kind of control proposed in the conclusion treats the issue of abortion and contraception only in its symbolic dimensions and frustratingly side-steps the very question the authors are, importantly, trying to raise. The originality of this contribution to the voluntary motherhood debate is not so much to rethink motherhood, but to rethink women's sexuality.

There is no doubt that pressure from feminist and other groups, plus women's courage in openly flouting the law and speaking out against the abortion law, were crucial to the eventual passing of the *loi Veil* in 1975, named after the then Minister of Health, Madame Simone Veil.[8] While the law did not abolish all legislation against abortion, it did make abortion legal in certain cases, with conscience clauses for the medical personnel involved, and with obstacles and cautions to women seeking abortion. For instance, abortions can only be performed by doctors in hospitals (which have the right to refuse abortion on the premises) on a woman whose pregnancy places her in a 'situation of distress'. The woman is informed of the risks of abortion; she is obliged to wait a week after her first request, in order to think it over (and preferably change her mind); and there is a ten-week limit imposed, after which abortion is again illegal.

The law was clearly unsatisfactory and did not allow for abortion to be reimbursed by Social Security (the French equivalent of the National Health system), which had been an important feminist demand. However, the very existence of the law altered the shape that feminist arguments about abortion took. Instead of demanding abortion as a right, women contested the limitations of the law. There was greater concentration on responses of individual women to the material conditions of abortion and criticism of hospital attitudes and treatment of women seeking abortion. The vitriolic condemnation of motherhood in capitalist society, making abortion a form of resistance to capitalism, is replaced by admission that the whole issue is more complex than at first appears, and there is more contemplation of the wider social and sexual significance of abortion.

Even so, the mobilising power of the abortion issue remained strong. The law had been voted for a trial period of five years and was due for re-discussion in the French parliament in 1979, for re-enactment or repeal in 1980. In spite of the fact that the original vigour of the early campaign had gone and the law was not what women wanted, the threat that it might be revoked brought 50,000 women out into the Paris streets on 6 October 1979 demonstrating in favour of the law.

Psych et Po remained conspicuously silent about abortion until they published a four-page article about it in 1979. Praising feminin-ity and rejecting masculinity as they did, pregnancy as an uncertain area in between would clearly pose a problem for them; and their declared opposition to legislative reform, perceived as desire to integrate into the masculine world, meant that they did not confront the question of the abortion law as other groups had done. The article, in the weekly *des femmes en mouvements* magazine (No. 4, p. 16, 1979), set out the group's attitude to abortion:

. . . mostly, abortion is necessary to show that there has been –
actually or symbolically – sexual violence – breaking and
entering, rape – . . . and to express and actively resist a macho
occupation of their whole body, right up to the uterus . . .
abortion rejects a repressive libidinal and political economy.

For *Psych et Po*, then, abortion is women's answer to male occupa-tion of their bodies. Its importance is, for them, symbolic, indicative of one means by which women can refuse to submit to the social and sexual constraints of patriarchy.

This campaign for free, legal abortion on demand, showed up from the first moments the differences of approach that divided the MLF. Questions of Left politics and feminism, class and sex, reformism and single issue campaigns, women's difference, capitalism and patriar-chy are all raised and given varying priority according to the interests of the group and also according to the evolution of the groups, and changing political attitudes to the issue in the wider context of French politics. It is possible to generalise, however, and say that at the beginning of the campaign, class struggle current analyses domin-ated, while at the end of the decade these had largely been absorbed by an approach more sharply focused on women themselves rather than on capitalism, while *Psych et Po* kept their own distance at all times. By 1979, the alteration of analysis showed a trend towards a less rigid approach to motherhood which many feminists found positive, a more honest blend of the personal and political aspects of women's lives. Others found that seeing the abortion issue in terms of women's individual experience had divested it of its original politically subversive content, and that the whole campaign had turned out to be a trap. They felt that the formula 'voluntary motherhood' reduced women's struggle for liberation to a question of providing individual women with means of choice over individual pregnancies rather than a question of a total re-evaluation of motherhood as a socially enforced role. Even worse, some felt that the campaign contributed to making those who 'chose' motherhood guilty: 'You wanted it, you enjoy it, so get on with it.' Which leads to the ironic equation 'enslaved motherhood + voluntary motherhood = voluntary slavery.'

The evolution of this feminist discussion can be explained by a combination of factors, internal and external to the MLF. As the first major campaign of the MLF, it attracted many women and was therefore important for its mobilising potential as well as for its centrality to analysis of women's oppression. Over the 1970s, the MLF moved away from the focus on capitalism as main source of oppression; once abortion had been legalised, the notion of choice, however limited, allowed women to consider motherhood in terms other than negative. The spread of psychoanalysis and increased interest in women's sexuality equally affected the way the abortion issue was perceived; and then the individual changes undergone by the women in the MLF were significant, for women have very different attitudes to motherhood when they are 20 and when they are 30. Finally, the evolution of the discussion on abortion reflects the collective transformation of the MLF, with the distinction becoming more acute between *Psych et Po* and other groups, and the difference between women who had identified as class struggle current feminists and non-aligned feminists becoming blurred.

The increased use of contraception and the legislation of abortion brought other, connected, issues to the foreground. For instance, women began to question their desire, or lack of desire, to have a child: contraception and conception are the two faces of the same coin, and once choice of conception is more or less possible, that choice must be faced. From the mid-1970s, there has been increased conviction that rejection of motherhood is not a satisfactory way of treating the issue, and would not solve the question of women's oppression. The tailoring of desire to the logic of politics is not always possible or acceptable.

Feminist texts on the desire for a child are obviously not couched in the same terms as the attack on the abortion law: there is no need to mobilise women, no campaign to be fought, but it is more a question of trying to explore experiences and feelings concerning an area that defies political analysis. This discussion has been very much the domain of non-aligned feminism, remaining outside the scope of class struggle current women and ignored by *Psych et Po*.

The women who formed groups to discuss this question found that they might try to disentangle culturally conditioned desires and 'real' desires, to find out what women's 'real' attitudes to motherhood were, but they couldn't actually do it.[9] They had to accept that social being and unconscious desires could not be separated, nor 'real' distinguished from socialist desires. Women's approach to their own attitudes and feelings abandoned any attempt to explain them, and concentrated on expressing them. One collection of articles, poetry, personal stories and fragmented thoughts on the subject[10] suggested for the first time that possibly the MLF had over-concentrated its energies on the denunciation of motherhood 'as if denunciation was the only way in which women could be subversive'.

It became acceptable to admit that not everything in our lives can be explained and analysed. Once the political nature of women's 'condition' had been accepted, in a sense proved, by feminists in the early 1970s, then it became important to re-establish desire as a part of any political analysis that claimed to base itself on women's lived experience. Feminists found themselves in the position of being able to have only those children they chose to have, to a great extent, and realised the evasive nature of desire. Not knowing what their desires actually were, many women were incapable of making a conscious decision about whether to have a child or not, and for many, ironically, the easiest way to deal with it was to act as if the choice did not exist at all.

Following on from this discussion, feminists also turned to explore feelings and experiences of pregnancy. Prior to feminist discussions, pregnancy had been a medical discourse with the pregnant women themselves seen as passive carriers of the all-important foetus, and the feminist discussion contributed to the de-medicalisation of the issue. In exploring their relation to their own, changed, bodies, women came up against the unforeseen problem of how to put bodily experience into language. The narcissism that often accompanies pregnancies, with concentration on the self and on the body, is most clearly evident in *Sorcières*. As a review that plays special attention to women's different voice, the connection between language and women's bodies, it had an interesting issue on pregnancy and childbirth (*Sorciéres* No. 4, *Enceintes, porter, accoucher*, p. 4, 1977) and focused on the difficulties of transforming experience into expression:

> . . . either women are the incarnation of 'natural' processes and find themselves treated as almost animal, wild and detached from society, lost in a dumb process of germination, splitting in two, burgeoning; the body is pure heaviness and language can only deform it. Or else pregnancy is inscribed into a mythical, hyper-ritualistic and cultural discourse; in this, the huge, painful body of the woman in labour, her labour, is hidden, and women are once again, silent.

When talking about childbirth, the range of tone and mode of discussion is wider and opinions are more extreme: childbirth is represented as either horror and violence, or as poetry. *Sorcières* again gives expression to the aestheticising of the experience (p. 16):

> the pocket that was the core explodes, such a tight, such a swollen sphere, the pocket explodes and, hot liquids drowning my thighs, suffering springs out of me.

More usual, however, in feminist discussion on childbirth, is to find that horror and violence dominate instead of poetry. One collection of articles, making up the dossier *Accouchement* (Giving Birth) in the journal *Le Temps des femmes* (No 4. 1979), was concerned to avoid the transformation from experience into text in their discussion. The women who transcribed their group discussion were concerned to keep in the weight of women's actual experience, and record women's feelings during pregnancy, before and after childbirth. The generally excited and positive approach to childbirth expressed before the event was regretted after it: women in the group almost all experienced childbirth as unfortunately negative, during which women lost such control as they had had before, or had hoped to have. All the women in the group spoke of feeling helpless in the face of pain, but beyond this, their experiences were all different and they did not try to draw any conclusions from the discussion. Their wish was simply 'to express the complexity and the many different ways in which women experience this moment'.

Questions féministes published a transcribed video (No 5, 1979), which had a far stronger stand on women's experience of childbirth, revealing uncompromisingly the violence done to women. Narrated by women accumulating their experiences, the stories combine to create a nauseating and terrifying picture of childbirth, showing how completely women's own words and feelings are ignored by the 'experts'. The narrative is interspersed with scientific and feminist texts, revealing the disparity between medical discourse and the woman's point of view about her own situation. The violence expressed is both physical, affecting women's bodies sometimes irrevocably, and psychological, depriving women in labour, frighteningly, of any sense of control over what is happening to them.

For *Psych et Po*, childbirth is the institutionalised torture of women. In their first newspaper, *Le Quotidien des femmes* (18 November 1975), doctors and midwives are represented as sadists and voyeurs, 'delegates of rapists, the father, the husband, the brother'. The woman is reduced to less than a body: 'the woman in labour is nothing but genitalia, made of muscular fibre which has to be sewn up by the medic on duty.' Childbirth is a game that a woman cannot win: if she shows her pain, she has failed in this age of natural, painless, childbirth; and if she is silent, she is the doctor's accomplice in his treatment of women.

The only positive form of childbirth for *Psych et Po*, is as metaphor, renamed a *mise au monde*, a 'bringing/coming to the world'. The birth metaphor is frequently used to describe intellectual production, which for them, replaces production of a child. Valuable creation is seen as the production of a text, a word, a woman's word, for in giving life to words, life is given to women, who write themselves into existence. Insistence on the symbolic dimension of childbirth shows the group's disregard for women whose production is reproduction. The important search for ways to put an imprint on the world has the reverse effect of negating any value of the way the majority of women live their lives.

The MLF, with its emphasis on women's own lives, women's

oppression, and basing its analysis on the oppressive nature of motherhood and the family, had no place for children: the MLF's early days absorbed women's entire lives, demanded total availability and, to a large extent, excluded mothers. With the MLF in a sense growing up, and the women involved growing older, and rethinking the first analyses of motherhood in the light of admission of newly-contradictory attitudes, feminists have more recently sought to change both the nature and the image of the mother role. They have thoroughly dissected the image of woman-as-mother in the search to prove that anatomy is not destiny. To this end, Freud's concept of female nature and his explanation of female sexual development have been attacked; and the various aspects of women's oppression entailed in motherhood – confinement to the home, exclusion from the non-domestic economy, isolation and dependence – have been explored. Yet women are not going to give up mothering, this much has always been clear, and so this role has to be made more acceptable:

a liberated motherhood, that is, freely taken on and fully erotic, that is, socially demanding, could alter social relations, alter the nature of work, eliminate the gap between private and public life, suggest a society constructed around mother and child, by and for, mothers and children.[11]

This vision of liberated motherhood suggests that reorganisation of the mother role could be truly revolutionary, with far-reaching consequences for social life generally. The question demanding exploration is that of women's identity in motherhood: how can women be mothers and still stay women?

Psych et Po (*des femmes en mouvements Hebdo* No. 30, 1979) contend that the woman is smothered by the mother:

What is a mother? What elements of woman-ness does it hide and oppress? either totally or at any rate enough so that an economic, political and symbolic system can feed off the mother to keep itself going, with the bosses exploiting the workers, the man-father exploiting the woman-mother, the name exploiting the body?

Others agree that motherhood suppresses femininity. Françoise Collin, in *Les Cahiers du GRIF* (No. 17–18, 1978) wrote that 'woman' as a concept is subversive, and that the threat of woman is defused upon motherhood. The image she conjures up is of a woman prowling around, captive within the mother, who is therefore not a genuine, feminine, mother, but an invention of the father: she is a 'mfather', who reinforces the father's authority. Collin attributes to mothers absorption into the father's values, which repress the feminine: the feminine is resistant, outside:

> woman is open, free, insolent, plural. The mother is full and keeps quiet. Men always try to put women into a maternal role, whether real or symbolic, thereby acknowledging women's alterity, their very threatening femininity.

Suggesting that the mother and father roles are the paradigm for all institutional and personal relations, these texts propose new models of motherhood which bear striking resemblance to the ideal of sisterhood:

> We have to replace the vertical and unilateral relation based on age and heritage . . . by a horizontal and reciprocal relation based on exchange, where we will find our mothers and our daughters on an equal basis.

This kind of motherhood is founded on complicity between women, and necessarily excludes men – the installation of horizontal, un-oppressive relationships eliminates the father as authority figure and changes the mother from being the father's accomplice to being 'other mothers, lightweight mothers, daughter mothers, sister mothers, carriers of an outlawed affection.' Sisterhood is, unproblematically, proposed as an alternative style of mothering which retains the subversive dimension of femininity.

Non-aligned feminists have also sought more realistic, more pragmatic ways of changing motherhood. By the end of the 1970s, early feminist rejection of motherhood was discarded: avoiding motherhood was no longer seen as the way to solve actual problems of power relations. These must instead be transformed, which will not happen 'by the silence of the children we do not have.'[12]

By the end of the 1970s, then, a whole range of questions involved in thinking about motherhood had been placed under scrutiny. The pre-feminist conceptualisation of motherhood as destiny and the early feminist notion of motherhood as slavery are equally rejected in the gradual understanding of the need to combine both choice and unconscious desires as well as working on the many contradictions inevitable in the personal/political equation, in any approach to motherhood.

Through looking at the way feminists have analysed motherhood, the interest and the shortcomings of the different MLF approaches are highlighted, the different preoccupations are evident and the evolution of the movement is reflected. Concentration on social aspects of motherhood, on the material conditions of motherhood in capitalism; discussion of only certain aspects of motherhood which fit into an analysis of women's difference; exploration of women's words, experiences – these reflect the priorities of the three major approaches within the MLF to this issue. Similar differences would be clear between the approaches in a discussion of women at work, or indeed in any 'topic' that has concerned feminists.

This diversity of style and approach is the MLF's strength, but also its weakness. While the tactical differences between groups mean that women can operate on different terrains and combine powerfully, it also means that no fundamental agreement over strategy can ever be reached. For every move made by one group, there will always be opposition from another: or the parallel actions will never be seen as part of the same struggle.

In a broader perspective, the trends detectable in feminist discussions on motherhood reflect changes detectable in the French Left, which has moved away from the revolutionary aspirations of May '68 and turned from the elaboration of analyses that incorporate and explain everything, towards a more cynical pragmatism, which translates as the desire to transform society as it is with the tools that are available. At the same time, the MLF approaches to motherhood show that from the outset, women seriously undertook the attempt to build up a body of feminist theory in which women's bodies and women's lives provide the starting point, in which theory and practice are answerable to each other, and which has already begun to challenge prevailing concepts of social relations, political activity and political thought.

CHAPTER 4

Feminists and (French) philosophy

In the chapters that follow, I want to turn the focus outwards, and make explicit the connection between feminism in France and its French context. This connection turns on the feminist insistence on 'difference' in its various meanings; whether in the *Psych et Po* sense of alterity – an innate, undiscovered femininity – or in the sense of wanting to change the procedures and contents of political activity as it exists in France.

In order to discuss this fully, two issues fundamental to feminism will be analysed in detail. Chapter 5 will take up the question of difference by looking at the concept of the feminine, as that which resists and challenges patriarchy in its discursive and psychological manifestation. Chapter 6 will follow through an examination of femin*ist* difference by discussing the case of feminists who attempt to locate a specifically feminist political practice that nevertheless exists within the traditional world of politics in France. This chapter asks the question: can feminists, with their different notions about political practice, intervene significantly in a political arena whose premises and imperatives are fundamentally incompatible with their own?

But first of all, I want to discuss the work of some of the major influences on feminist thinking in France which will explain the French feminist concern with difference – by which most anglophone feminists remain unmoved. French feminism owes much to different intellectual currents of post-war France. In the constant attempt to understand the female subject's situation in society and develop strategies for change, feminists have used psychoanalytic explanations of the constitution of the subject; linguistic and philo-sophical critiques of the production of meaning; critiques of power, and the role of theory as justification for, and support of, domination – not only domination in the concrete sense, but also, for some more importantly, domination of discursive practices.

In the building of new feminist theory, a complex web of influ-ences is visible. As in the experience of the MLF as a political move-ment, some elements in feminist thinking are consonant with other aspects of French cultural and political life, while others break completely from it; some feminist thinkers transform the work of others, for feminist purposes, while others locate their own work within the scope of existent theory. This chapter will explore the French intellectual climate in which contemporary feminism emerged, and look specifically at thinkers whose work has first been taken up, and later challenged, by feminists in France.

Pragmatic British and American feminists frequently find the interest in philosophy displayed by French feminists somewhat irrelevant and hyper-intellectual, but it must not be forgotten that philosophy plays a different role in French society from its role both in Britain and the United States. The French school student has a compulsory class in philosophy and can be examined in philosophy when she leaves school. The French lycée pupil therefore has a familiarity with certain philosophical ideas and thinkers that the British or American child lacks; the French child is also subjected to oral examinations and gains practice in argument and rhetoric; and the institutionalising of philosophy affects the degree of importance allocated to abstract inquiry, and the relative importance of intellec-tual life in France compared to British anti-intellectualism.

Nor is philosophy divorced from politics. Alongside the 'official' philosophy taught in schools and universities has grown a philo-sophical tradition associated with the Left, with its theoretical con-tent directly connected to its political goals. This connection was highlighted by the events of May '68. May '68 challenged the institutional transmission of meaning, and opened a connection between psychoanalysis and radical political thinking; and the criti-que of power undertaken by philosopher Michel Foucault, for instance, blurred the distinction between philosophy and politics.

The intellectual context of French feminism has mirrored the political context in that it too has an anti-authority and anti-hierarchy focus. In philosophical terms, this means not questioning the relation of state and civil society, or the deficiencies of political parties, but attacking the authority of meaning and the systems of domination and exclusion that underpin political authority. To the ultimate set of norms and values that exists in every society, feminism opposes otherness – alterity – and multiplicity, and suggests that a plurality of modes of thought is both possible and preferable to the monolithic, monological masculinity that dominates in patriarchy. To this extent, feminism in France has been bathed in the philosophical ambience of those thinkers whose work examines language as a non-transparent and therefore active medium for social interaction; who investigate the meaning of the social subject; who examine the foundations of philosophy; and who show the interconnections between knowledge, power and language. When combined with the extra-parliamentary culture of protest in France, the added influence of American feminism (French women read, for instance, Betty Friedan and Kate Millett), and the presence of French *Féministes Révolutionnaires* at the founding conference of the British women's liberation movement at Ruskin College, Oxford in 1970, the whole adds up to a courageous and powerfully heterogeneous body of thinking and practices.

The influence of certain French thinkers is clearest in the work of individual feminist intellectuals, and in the orientations of *Psych et Po*. Non-aligned feminists emphasise experience as the valid starting point for theoretical endeavour; women engage with the work of, for instance, Jacques Lacan, but do not directly and specifically base their own thinking on acceptance or rejection of a Lacanian model of social relations. Women who give pride of place to the Marxism/ feminism connection, either before, during or after the short life of the class struggle current, or inside political parties, have followed the example of many Communist intellectuals and developed their own Marxism outside the confines of the French Communist Party (PCF). Because of the PCF's theoretical rigidity and practical insufficiencies, these women have returned to the founding texts – Marx, Engels and later Lenin and Bebel – to try to develop a feminist Marxism rather than adhering to party pronouncements on women. The institutionalised nature of Marxism in France, in the PCF, has strongly affected the contours of this feminist attempt. New theoretical enterprise has to be defined in relation to the party, which does not admit of dialogue or dissent from within. Any theory that emerges is limited, restricted by the women's relation to their party.

Innovative theory therefore tends to be elaborated by those who have rejected their party outright and retain no ambivalence either about their affiliation or about the men they left behind.

I will concentrate here on those thinkers whose double-fronted attack on the stability of meaning and the philosophical destruction of the stable self, has had an active, positive effect on feminist thinking. The discussion will focus on the trends of the last twenty years – semiology, deconstruction and Lacanian psychoanalysis – that have contributed to the shaping of French feminist theory, with the shared preoccupation with identity and difference, exclusion and repression, and the role of language.

Roland Barthes, and particularly Michel Foucault and Jacques Derrida have all been concerned with the underside, with the outside, of the Western, male, logocentric system that has dominated Western thought since the time of the ancient Greeks. These thinkers are not in search of an all-encompassing explanation of the world, but seek to show how hierarchy of meaning is created, and how meaning is always, inevitably linked to power relations. Apparently limpid, uncomplicated phenomena are scrutinised in order to see the conditions of their production, their significance and their relation to other phenomena. Nothing is now accepted as innocent.

Feminist concern with otherness, feminine difference, is in keeping with the recent French philosophical tradition which, as the title of a recently published overview of French philosophy indicates (*Le Même et l'autre*/The Same and the Other) has been dominated by questions of identity and perception. Otherness, or alterity, in French philosophy, has two, connected meanings: the 'other' as in a relation to the speaking subject (a tradition in which Simone de Beauvoir placed her work, discussing woman as socially defined, as inessential, the other to man's subjectivity, and in which we also find Hegel and Sartre, and phenomenologists Husserl and Heidegger); and 'otherness' extended to encompass that which is outside a dominant conceptual system. For instance, madness, poetry, cannibalism, could be seen as psychological, linguistic and social otherness. Otherness does not subscribe to an identifiable set of norms, values and practices that the Western Judeo-Christian world can assimilate and understand.[1]

Certain feminists, combining philosophical and psychoanalytical insights and political goals, have appropriated otherness and assimilated it to the feminine, and in this, have moved away from Simone de

Beauvoir's existentialist use of the word. De Beauvoir posed the problem of being a woman, of being other, in terms of 'this conflict between the fundamental needs of every subject who always sees herself as essential, and the demands made on her by her situation, which constitutes her as inessential.'[2] De Beauvoir confronts the question of women's experience contrasted with the demands of society, which imposes a different image on her from the image she has of herself. For de Beauvoir, and for radical feminists such as the *Questions Féministes* collective, if women are other it is because they have been defined as other by men, and 'other' means 'inferior'. In contrast to this, feminist thinkers such as Hélène Cixous and Luce Irigaray perceive otherness, the feminine, in terms of understanding the dominant discursive parameters of our time. The coming to life of the feminine would necessarily alter the way we think, open up new possibilities and make oppression in social discursive practices no longer an inevitability.

In a rather schematic way, then, I want to pick out those elements of recent French theory that have contributed actively to feminist thinking about otherness. In the case of semiology, this has been the investigation into cultural myths and codes, the process of social 'demythification' such as that undertaken by Roland Barthes in his early collection of essays, *Mythologies*. Semiology, like Marxism but without the Marxist claim of providing an alternative vision, strips away layers of 'reality' to reveal the power of the hidden. Semiology, the science of signs at work in society, tells the observer about the values and priorities of a culture, by taking apart the givens of that culture and analysing the implications and significance of even the most seemingly innocuous sign. Semiology therefore makes a political point. Barthes calls the semiologist of cultural myths a mythologist, and assigns to himself, as mythologist, the task of disrupting the surface of things, the surface of order and innocence, to reveal the conflict beneath. In 1957, when Barthes wrote *Mythologies*, he attacked the apparently apolitical, neutral world of the French bourgeoisie. He looks at such French cultural national institutions as the cover of *Paris Match*, or the bicycle race, the *Tour de France*, or the mythology of *Steak-frites* in order to explore the mechanisms of bourgeois French values and culture. Feminists look at pornography, advertising and the beauty industry to show the mechanisms of misogynistic patriarchal culture.

71

The myth is the commonplace, seemingly innocent assumption that has unacknowledged, unexplained ideological roots. The myth shifts its subject from the temporal, historical plane to the static, eternal plane; it doesn't explain, it simply presents; it wipes out contradiction and depth. Things seem to be invested with meaning all by themselves, without that meaning ever having been created in the first place, put there by some one, something, for some reason.

Barthes' focus, then, is on the trappings of bourgeois culture, yet semiology can allow for any focus. Feminist interest in myth is clearly in the myth of Woman, as a natural, eternal being; naturally inferior to men, naturally destined to be wife and mother, madonna or whore. Feminists have focused on aspects of society that perpetuate these images of women to show how there is nothing natural and eternal about them.

Michel Foucault, like Barthes, has not been so much a direct influence on French feminist theory, but has been equally instrumental in creating the atmosphere in which theory in France is produced. It is no exaggeration to say that, until his recent death, Foucault occupied the position of the foremost thinker in France, whose words were paid unparalleled attention. Attending his lectures at the Collège de France was an experience as much to watch the responses of the faithful as to hear what he had to say.[3] Foucault's hypothesis was that the relations and strategies of power, which constitute and permeate the human subject, produce and are accompanied by forms of knowledge and truth that sustain them and make them seem natural; the forms of truth conceal the domination and violence inherent in power formations. Truth, for Foucault, can only be understood as 'a system of ordered procedures for the production, regulation, distribution, circulation and operation of statements'.[4] 'Truth' and 'knowledge' cannot therefore be considered as disinterested, abstract categories independent of history.

Foucault's writings have examined the nature of the solidarity between knowledge and power, both in abstract and in specific terms. Looking at the organisation of knowledge and at the production of meaning, Foucault has studied the discourses of exclusion and repression that have made the dominance of certain meanings possible. Operating from the understanding that the object of a particular discourse is never the real reason for that discourse, Foucault examines the likely reasons behind the production of different discourses. For instance, he has looked at medicine, madness, incarceration and sexuality to analyse the way in which these objects have been constructed and why. 'Woman' is not the primary concern of the ways in which people talk about 'woman': this too is a discourse created by and for others.

Like Barthes, Foucault rejects the idea of the innocent, passive existence of knowledge, of language, and like him sought to disturb the surface of tranquillity that hides the procedures that allow this surface to appear in the first place:

> . . . all these syntheses that are accepted without question, must remain in suspense. They must not be rejected definitively of course, but the tranquillity with which they are accepted must be disturbed; we must show that they do not come about of themselves, but are always the result of a construction, the rules of which must be known, and the justifications of which must be scrutinized . . .[5]

Foucault's work shows how difference is repressed, and shows up the nonsense of essentialist arguments. As such, and as the rigorous examination of the production of knowledge, it is of clear interest to feminists in the struggle against prevailing arguments about women's place. Indeed, one way of looking at the entire feminist theoretical enterprise would be to see it as the examination of the construction of woman as object of discourse – and the reorientation of this discourse to create a new object – women – with women themselves as the reason behind the discourse.

Barthes' and Foucault's work are two examples of French philosophical work that has influenced feminist thinking through its influence on the French intellectual scene in general, rather than as specific named sources. The influence of the other two philosophers to be discussed here – Jacques Derrida and Jacques Lacan – are both more pervasive and more specific: specific in the sense that the influence is extremely clear within individual feminist's work, and pervasive because Derrida's and Lacan's concepts and ideas have served as a framework in which certain feminists have located their own reflection, and which, in various ways, they later challenge.

Jacques Derrida, in his work, undertakes a critique of Western metaphysics with which many feminist thinkers strongly identify, at least up to a point. Metaphysics can be defined as the belief in a reality external to discourse that can be described and represented. In other words, belief in a world where things are really there and are what they seem; where people can be described as being 'happy', or 'sad' or whatever, and where we can understand and grasp things for what they are, ideas and people as well. We live in a metaphysical world and assumptions about meaning and identity are necessary for us to get by. Derrida looks to find the 'origins' of metaphysical thinking, and to this end, looks at Plato's *Phaedrus* and what is said there about language. In a metaphysical thought system, oral speech is contrasted with writing at the expense of the latter. Oral speech, or the Logos, the father's spoken word, is believed to remain interior to the soul when uttered, and is therefore at one with meaning. Writing, on the other hand, is condemned for distancing language from the soul, thereby exposing meaning to the dangers of interpretation: meaning would apparently be intrinsic to the spoken word, while it can be imposed by the reader on writing. This, Derrida claims, is crucial for the way the Western world thinks about language: speech is considered to be the practically transparent transmission of thought, able to be grasped in its reality by the listener, while writing is only the representation of representation (the phrase belongs to Jonathan Culler[6]) as words represent something else, and writing represents words.

Derrida holds that metaphysics is predicated on a false assumption: that this true, self-identical meaning is possible in the first place; that we can instantly, or ever, grasp the essence of a thing in itself in its integrity. As soon as there is meaning at all, for Derrida, there is difference; as soon as we describe or identify something, there is spacing, distancing. This diacritical gap is intrinsic to knowledge whether written or spoken – spoken language is inhabited by the same elements of difference and spacing as written language. For Derrida, there is no possibility of grasping the essence of an object, a concept, a person, in an unmediated way – we pass through language, and language creates a mediated meaning. From here, he goes on to conclude that there is in fact nothing to grasp in the first place, no reality that exists but we simply cannot apprehend in its integrity (which would be the equivalent of Lacan's *Réel*), no reality outside discourse, leading to his well-known aphorism that there is nothing outside the text.

The metaphysical error of assuming that Being is determined by being there, by presence, has affected the entire conceptual system of the Western world. Presence, or Being, is contrasted to absence, and all categories of thought are divided into either/or binary oppositions: man/woman, culture/nature, good/evil, speech/writing, raw/cooked, etc. Each of these pairs has the first term valued at the expense of the second, and each is implicit when thinking about either of the terms.

Derrida's notion of *différance*[7] upsets this hierarchy, upsets the idea that something exists prior to differences, something exists in and of itself, as origin, as giver of meaning, as 'transcendental signified', explaining and organising/ordering everything else. *Différance* disturbs, for in Derrida's view, almost all post-Kantian philosophy has had the aim of seeking this ultimate source of explanation of the world, and this search has systematically repressed difference.

It is precisely to reveal the differences, the inherent ambiguity, the lack of authority, the polysemantic possibilities of a text (and anything can be considered as a text), that Derrida undertakes the process of deconstructive readings. Deconstruction questions the presuppositions, the assumptions on which a text is based; the starting-point of any text is questioned as are those elements that affect the text without necessarily being visible in the text. What is at stake is not the meaning of a text, but the conditions of that text's production. Derrida's concern is not to 'prove wrong' what is written in any text, but to show how the primacy of one meaning in the text is created by the suppression of others. This approach to the text reveals the absence of an ultimate reference or 'transcendental signified', and posits that there is never any conclusive determination of meaning, but an infinite play of interpretations.

For Derrida, there are no fixed meanings, no absolutes, no stable identities. If meaning is created through language – sound and mark (signifiers), and reference (signifieds) – then it is created through differentiation; components of language and the things behind the words are meaningless in isolation. This abolition of fixed meaning makes nonsense of our binary conceptual system: the terms referred to depend on the belief in immobile, immutable meaning. If 'presence', being, does not in and of itself mean something, and mean it once and for all time, then 'absence' is rendered as floating a term as presence, and they cannot be set up in opposition to each other.

The connections between Derrida's work and feminist theory become clear when this logocentric way of ordering the world is inextricably bound up, as it is in much feminist theorising, with masculinity and the dominance of the Phallus. Derrida's critique hints at ways that difference – in this case the feminine – can be *thought* in a way not tied to the negative pole of a binary opposition (masculine/feminine); it leaves open the possibility for other forms of thought to exist, even if we have not yet reached the point where we can identify these other forms, or use them.

Derrida himself is sceptical about ever reaching this point, about the possibility of going beyond metaphysical thought and making new kinds of meaning. This means finding new ways of making sense of experience, as, so far, metaphysical thinking and language is the only way we possess. It means an upheaval in our forms of thought and expression that is disturbing even to imagine, though exciting in its vision of untapped possibilities. What Derrida does propose is a kind of resistance from within: resistance can only ever be from within if it uses language,[8] but certain strategies of writing can practise distancing nevertheless. The logocentric desire for unity, authorship and one meaning only in a text can be upset by a writing that suggests a plurality of authorship, multiple meanings, contradictory styles, punctuation that upsets syntax and forces the reader to arrest her assumptions about meaning.

Derrida's project complements the work of Foucault. Banishing the ultimate giver of meaning, the 'transcendental signified', he upsets the status of philosophy, from being a meta-discourse, disinterested commentary on the world and explicator of the world, and the search for Truth, Knowledge and Being, into simply another type of text, another genre to be analysed. The deconstruction of philosophy as meta-discourse paves the way for understandings about the way that philosophy and systems of knowledge have themselves been constructed, within certain constraints and parameters. In this, and in the discrediting of logocentrism, Derrida's work has been instrumental in feminist formulations of a quest for a feminine principle that upsets and unsettles the order installed by metaphysics.

Where the paths diverge, however, is over the potential for escape from metaphysics. Derrida does not set out a programme for a new, discursive future, but is pointing out that things are not there by themselves, we do not think as we do because it is the natural way to think, and the kind of resistance to metaphysics that he proposes through deconstruction, through writing practices, will make us more aware of the ways in which meanings come about. Feminists who have worked from Derridean premises, however, do seem to think that eventually there could be another way of thinking, one that includes the feminine and therefore, necessarily, destroys logocentrism and masculine domination.

The attention paid to Derrida by feminists in France is also given to Lacan, with the same disagreements. The general schema of thought proposed by both men is not challenged by feminists, but what is ultimately challenged is the limits of the conclusions that both men draw. For Derrida, logocentrism is inevitable; for Lacan, the Phallus will always dominate. Feminists have rejected this closure which infinitely maintains a conceptual system that excludes and represses the feminine.

Jacques Lacan occupied a special place in French intellectual life, intersecting as he did in his work the two areas of theoretical inquiry both prominent and fashionable in France: psychoanalysis and language. French intellectuals all have an opinion about Lacan, whether at the level of absorbing stock phrases (such as the unconscious being structured like a language), or at the level of a serious consideration of his rather precious style. Psychoanalysis has been associated with philosophy by the importance placed on language in both 'fields', and with the political Left since May '68. Sociologist Sherry Turkle suggests that one reason for this association was the fact that French medical institutions long resisted psychoanalysis as a valid scientific enterprise.[9] However, psychoanalysis appealed to the surrealists and the avant-garde in pre-war Paris and, Turkle suggests, the inclusion in artistic, anti-institutional circles meant that psychoanalysis in France has been invested with philosophical and ideological significance that has not been the case elsewhere.

May '68 also opened new ways for psychoanalysis to be received: during the events, the challenge to boundaries of all kinds included that of the distinction between the personal and the political. Lacan's model of society offered a view that the individual is inhabited by society through language, and the new awareness of the political nature of private life meant that psychoanalysis, as discourse of the unconscious, attracted new interest. Lacanian analysis in particular, in helping the analysand come to terms with the loss and lack inherent in subjecthood, rather than trying to fit her/him into a social structure in need of radical change evidently appealed to left-wing sympathisers; the Lacanian description of the subject as lack (*manque-à-être*) mirrors, on a personal scale, alienation in capitalist society.

For feminists, who insist on the connection between the social and the sexual, psychoanalysis and its work on the construction of subjectivity and on female psychosexual development would obviously provoke a variety of responses, and Lacan, as the 'French Freud' would inevitably provide the focus for French feminists. Lacanian analysis, in emphasising the role of language in the structuring of the social subject, is of particular interest to feminists, for, as Jane Gallop and Carolyn Burke have said, psychoanalysis can uncover the working upon us and within us of patriarchy as discourse.[10] Lacan's description of the child's accession to social subjecthood provides a fruitful model for feminists, concerned with the female experience of, and relation to, subjecthood in a society founded on and by the Western male thought and word.

From Claude Lévi-Strauss, Lacan borrows the idea that all societies are regulated by a series of signs, roles and rituals which have meaning only in relation to each other, forming recognisable codes and expressed in language. Lacan calls this 'the Symbolic Order', which is always already in place in society, and must be accepted and internalised by the child in order to function adequately as a social subject; and at the same time as the child internalises, unconsciously, these sets of rules of language and behaviour, she or he is produced by them at the level of the unconscious. The Symbolic Order is not arbitrary, cannot be chosen or disregarded at will, is not set up by accident. It is dependent on the law which founds society: for Lévi-Strauss, this was the law of incest, which Lacan translates into the 'Law of the Father', represented by the authority invested in his name and his power to forbid (his *nom* and his *non*). The father represents society's laws, and the acceptance of his authority is essential for the 'normal' development of the child. This acceptance, which takes place through the resolution of the Oedipus complex, marks the child's entry into the Symbolic and becoming a subject capable of functioning and participating in the Symbolic Order. The child's subjecthood is constructed by, and operates within, the Symbolic Order which has been unconsciously accepted, and just as this Symbolic Order structures his conscious being, so it structures his unconscious.[11]

Feminists have used this description as a starting point for reflection on women's specific place within, or in relation to, the Symbolic, and also for thinking about the discovery, uncovering, of the feminine, which has been repressed. Some feminists focus on the way that the conceptualisation of the child's entry into the Symbolic is modelled on the boy's experience of the Oedipal situation and ignores the little girl's passage through this crisis, assuming it to be identical to the boy's. Women are said by some to be excluded from the Symbolic and live in a world that is, at a most fundamental level, not theirs. Others have given a different attention to the Symbolic, starting from the observation that the Symbolic Order, founded on the Father's Law, is thus always patriarchal, and, working at the level of the unconscious as it does, brings the little girl into unconscious structures that are always masculine, and represses her (and his) femininity, which never is, and never can be, expressed: the tools needed for it to come into existence are lacking.

Lacan's model provides *Psych et Po* with a conceptual framework from which they elaborate a theory of the feminine. Unlike Lacan, they believe that the feminine can be defined and brought into an existence that defies the Symbolic Order. Close scrutiny of Lacan's texts has fuelled feminist approaches to the exclusion of the feminine, has propelled women to seek in the founding texts of the contemporary Western world the ways in which women have been ignored, repressed or excluded, and how masculinity at a conceptual level denies the feminine.[12]

Lacan says very little actually about women. In his oblique way, with throw-away asides and occasionally acute comments, he says that 'woman' is an unknown quantity. His famous comment that woman does not exist, refers to his suggestion, which many feminists have taken up, that woman as a concept cannot be universally defined and thereby limited; and refers to his insistence that woman as a concept can never come into existence because the Oedipus complex brings the little girl into masculine unconscious structures and that, because they are created by acceptance of patriarchal law, these structures will always remain masculine. This is further suggested by Lacan's discussion on defining woman, suggesting that woman is outside – beyond – the conceptual imagination of phallic discourse, which limits and circumscribes all that it touches. The feminine cannot be definitively defined and therefore cannot be captured and pinned down.

In stating that woman has not been conceptualised, Lacan finds agreement among feminists. The paths diverge over whether or not it is possible to conceptualise woman at all, and if so, how to do it. Lacan says that it can't be done; but feminist theorists are not satisfied with leaving attempts at characterising woman as the negative of the phallic. Starting from this negative position, feminists have been seeking to define woman *provisionally* as something else, as outside the conceptual scheme of phallic, logocentric thought, in possession of a different economy, unknown but not always condemned to remaining unknowable.

For Lacan, woman is irreducibly, unknowably Other, as mystically Other as God:

. . . it became clear that the supreme Being, which is manifestly mythical in Aristotle, the immobile sphere from which originate all movements, whether changes, engenderings, movements, translations or whatever, is situated in the place, the opaque of the *jouissance* of the Other – that Other which, if she existed, the woman might be.[13]

Otherness in general, and the feminine in particular, is placed in opposition to the thinking subject endowed with a coherent identity, placed in a potentially different discursive structure: woman is situated as opposition to Descartes' *cogito* and we, ranged alongside the *cogito*, cannot apprehend or imagine it.

Any attempt at defining woman, provisionally, must begin with sexual pleasure, *jouissance*.[14] For Lacan, this is where the difference of libidinal economy, difference in the way energy is organised and spent, begins. Feminine *jouissance* is outside phallic description: it is a kind of pleasure about which nothing is known precisely because the language that could begin to describe it is lacking within the bounds of phallic discourse. This different *jouissance*, different sexual economy, is always foreclosed through the resolution of the Oedipus complex and can only be hinted at, imagined (and maybe not even that, at least not in words); the feminine, which – if allowed to exist – would change the world, can never exist except at the level of potentiality and can never develop into anything else. Lacan does not attempt to disturb this foreclosure, or condemn it, but attributes to it the exclusion of woman from the Symbolic.

Lacan reinforces the case for otherness in his theory of subjectivity, in which Man is moved away from the centre of the stage, no longer in control of his own destiny, nor in possession of a non-alienated self. Alienation develops at the same time as, and as an integral part of, the identity of the human subject. This occurs through the 'mirror stage', in which the child perceives itself as exterior, perceives an image that is apparently coherent and solid in a way that contrasts utterly with its interior sensations in looking at itself. For Lacan, the subject is defined as lack, lack of being, or as a want-to-be (*manque-à-être* means both of these). The subject perpetually seeks recognition from another subject, needs to be seen as subject; identity must be proven by this recognition, but the other's response is always ambiguous (there can be no certainty as to the nature of the other's recognition – the other may not be sincere) and so the subject can never be really reassured about its identity. Lacan's anxious human subject, with its imaginary relations and empty core, imprinted by the world through language, is far from the notion of true self-identity and the autonomous, intentional human subject always at the heart of Western thought. The dethroning of Man, deconstruction of the centre and reassertion of alterity has provided fertile ground for feminist explorations into female subjectivity, sexuality and social role, not only by *Psych et Po*, but by many others.

It must be said that not all feminist groups display the same fascination for Lacanian theory as *Psych et Po*. But it must not be forgotten that in France, philosophical thinking has wider currency, has a more positive reception than it does in English-speaking countries. It is more than a fad, more than a fashionable surface: Lacan's suggestions about social organisation and the Symbolic, and the impossibility of conceptualising the feminine, have clearly touched a chord of recognition in many feminists.

The philosophical climate in France of the 1960s and 1970s has been particularly fruitful for feminists, with the critiques of discursivity, power and subjectivity informing and guiding their own work. The coincidence of feminism and recent French philosophical directions has created a feminist attempt to reorientate the destabilisation of meaning and of identity in a way that can be favourable to women: for if, as is believed, women have always been excluded from the Symbolic, with the feminine libidinal economy always closed off before it is ever allowed to exist, many feminists simply do not accept that this is as inevitable as Lacan assumes, and have been working to understand how this exclusion has been effected and how it can be overcome. They have been engaged in attempts to bring the feminine into existence, and are seeking ways in which the authoritarian, phallocentric and logocentric Symbolic Order can be irrevocably disrupted.

81

CHAPTER 5

The concept of the feminine

What has this disruption been? How have understandings about unconscious and conceptual structures affected feminist politics and given feminists new insights?

The ambivalent relationship of feminism to theory in general calls for comment. A movement that bases its analysis on women's own experience and perceives the world as constructed by and for men will, to some extent, see theory as support for the seeking and maintaining of power. Non-aligned feminism tends to be suspicious of over-arching, generalising tendencies, mistrusting abstractions and perceiving theory as a dimension of male repression, as justification of the violence inherent in rationality. As Rosi Braidotti says, feminism often considers theory to be 'a power strategy whose objective is to support and justify the social practice of the oppression of women.'[1]

Questions Féministes (No.1, 1977) saw theory as something necessary for women to use for their own benefit:

A theoretical discourse, whatever its language, is a discourse that attempts to explain the causes and the mechanisms, the why and the how of women's oppression in general or of one of its specific aspects; it is any discourse that tries to draw political conclusions, which suggests a strategy or tactics for the feminist movement.

Theory, then, can be a tool for women's political purposes as much as for men's; and feminist theory has the obligation to disentangle the threads of women's oppression, and by revealing the 'hows' and the 'whys', to begin to undo it. *Psych et Po* too, but differently, thought of theory as something for women to use. Antoinette Fouque described *Psych et Po's* approach in an interview with Catherine Clément in *Le Matin*, 16 July 1980:

> we wanted *Psych et Po* to be a laboratory for understanding the impasses of the May Movement and the women's movement (as all movements develop, there are elements which remain unthought). For our work on this lack of conceptualisation, lack of consciousness, we make use of current instruments of thought, particularly of psychoanalysis, which is the only discourse on sexuality available at this time.

Whatever the particular focus, feminists seem to agree that new theory, new in substance and in approach, must be formulated, and that 'old' theory can be usefully pillaged, reassessed, reworked, subverted. Theory is not a set of fixed references, but is dynamic, a tool to be used for feminist purposes. For *Psych et Po*, this means finding ways to 'bring the feminine into existence', while for the MLF *non-déposé*, it means seeking ways to analyse and demystify patriarchy and to project a reconstruction of a society where relations of domination are eliminated. Rather than tending towards one, final, feminist theory, the approaches will remain multiple and diverse in orientation. Feminists borrow freely from any thinker whose work could be useful, extracting those elements they want to use and discarding the rest. As suggested in Chapter 4, two major influences have been Derrida and Lacan, although they are by no means the only influences.

The fact that I will concentrate here on a discussion of one particular aspect of feminist theory must not be taken as an indication that this is the only, or the 'most important' feminist theoretical investigation. I do think, however, that this challenge to patriarchy as discourse – phallogocentrism – is somewhat alien to English-speaking feminists, grounded in a different theoretical tradition, and having different implications for feminist politics which are most in evidence in France, and as such, is worth special attention.

Penser autrement, thinking differently, is a dream and a project, expressed by those feminists who concentrate on examining how patriarchy works on us as a misogynistic discourse. Patriarchy is not only a political and social system that exploits and oppresses women from outside, in concrete visible ways; it inhabits the individual through language, through the metaphysical, logocentric conceptual structures in which we necessarily think. The term 'phallocentric' is ascribed to this manifestation of patriarchy as discourse, often assimilated with logocentrism, to form the neologism 'phallogo-centrism'. In this term, the Phallus and the Logos combine to form one, discursive, Symbolic enemy against which the feminine, as incarnation of all that resists, must struggle.

It is suggested by feminist theorists who have worked primarily from Derridean and Lacanian premises that the advent of the femi-nine, towards which they are working, could destroy Judeo-Christianity and Western metaphysics as the discursive parameters of our time. Those engaged in the quest for the feminine hope that their work will pave the way for the oppressive binary logic of meta-physical thinking to be undone, and for new ways of perceiving and expressing alterity, difference, in a way not dependent on identifica-tion with the Phallus and the Logos (the father), to be made possible. Feminists therefore combine their theoretical investigations with their political interests and challenge their philosophical masters. These French feminist theorists posit that there could be a 'beyond', an 'elsewhere', an as yet unrealised potential for new meanings and a new relation between gender, signifying and representation, and that it is clearly in women's interests that this potential be realised.

The concern with epistemology and psychoanalysis that this leads to, appears highly abstract, and women may wonder what exactly it all has to do with our lives. 'Everything,' would be the response of the French theorists – including providing the basis upon which to build a revolutionary strategy. It is as important to dismantle the givens of phallogocentric discourse as it is to demystify the structures of patriarchy – it is the same process but in a different domain. Phal-logocentrism is insidious, working upon men and women through the unconscious, through cultural habits, working from within as well as from without. The examination of these processes by femin-ists with the ultimate goal of disrupting them is essential before practices to effect this disruption could be embarked on, let alone achieved. The work of, for instance, Hélène Cixous, Luce Irigaray and Julia Kristéva reminds us that our entire cultural framework is predicated on the indifferentiation of gender, on the repression/

suppression of the feminine. *Psych et Po's* project has been specifically named 'the Revolution of the Symbolic' (so named by themselves), a revolution to bring about the existence of the feminine, while the three theorists named above have concentrated in their different ways on women's relation to language, theory and sexuality, and from these connections, have made tentative speculations about the feminine.

The major concern of these three women theorists is the repression, the exclusion of feminine difference in phallogocentric (white, male, metaphysical) culture. Using arguments also formulated by Lacan and Derrida, each has gone beyond the men they started with/from, each suggesting ways to challenge the inevitability of patriarchy, in discursive and conceptual terms as much as in terms of social structure.

In response to Lacan's account of the child's psychosexual development, the question posed by Julia Kristéva is: where is the place of woman in his schema? Her own answer is that woman is that which cannot be represented in the Symbolic, cannot be conceived of, or be present within it. Woman is always negative, against what *is* present in the Symbolic; always protesting that it isn't there, it isn't this (can't be defined), it isn't yet that (isn't yet here). It is outside the system that names and that imposes order and explanation. The feminist is therefore absent from the Symbolic, as it is in Lacan's view. This Kristéva sees as due to the way the child in the Oedipal phase, must reject (if a girl) or repress (if a boy) desire for the mother's body in order to be able to identify herself/himself through language and the father. Kristéva locates the feminine in the pre-Oedipal phase, and describes its effect in language as semiotic (her own use of the word), which she places in opposition to the Symbolic. Kristéva describes the Symbolic as: 'that which, in language, includes all that is sign, that is, at the same time, naming, syntax, meaning and denotation of an "object" first, or of a scientific truth afterwards.'[2] Her notion of the Symbolic, then, is Lacanian. But rather than contrast it with the two other registers, of the Real (that which Lacan suggests exists but which we can never grasp because it always remains outside discourse) and the Imaginary (the register in which we convince ourselves of the illusion that there are fixed meanings and stable identities), Kristeva contrasts it with the semiotic, which precedes and underlies it. The semiotic is 'chronologically anterior to, and synchronically transversal to, the sign, to syntax, to denotation and to meaning. Made by openings and the marks they leave, the semiotic is a provisional articulation, a non-expressive rhythm.' In adult language, the semiotic is more or less repressed, but erupts into the Symbolic as 'rhythm, prosody, word games, meaninglessness, laughter', from its place in the unconscious, to which, through the resolution of the Oedipus complex, it has been repressed.

For Kristéva, the subversive nature of the semiotic lies in its contradiction with, its disruption of, the Symbolic. At no time does she suggest that the latter should or could be replaced by the former. The power of the semiotic lies in its fragmented, occasional, provisional presences within the Symbolic, thus challenging the limits of representation and the order installed by the Symbolic. Kristéva's notion of the feminine belongs – with the languages of madness, the irrational, the maternal and the sexual – to the semiotic, and can have an undermining effect on the power of the Symbolic from its position as marginal, but never leaving this position. She describes the relation of the semiotic to the Symbolic:

. . . while there is no practice without *doxa* or without a *thesis*, these are simply repetitive systems without the heterogeneous contradictions of the semiotic, which, by its cycle of appearance, displaces infinitely and minutely the *thesis*, the signifiable and signifying *being*; which means that this heterogeneous contradiction of the semiotic is the very mechanism of renewal. The semiotic is only revolutionary when it confronts the symbolic *thesis*.

The confrontation of the two reveals the gaps in the control of the Symbolic and points to the undermining potential of other discourses.

Kristéva is careful to distinguish between the masculine and the feminine, and biological men and women; if the child has the possibility, upon entry into the Symbolic, of identifying with either the mother or the father, and if the extent of his/her masculinity or femininity depends on the extent of the identification, then children of both sexes have the same unconscious choices open to them. It would be dangerous to collapse the discursive into the biological: this is precisely what patriarchy does, locking men and women into roles and attributes with reference to some constructed ideal of masculinity and femininity. The identification will determine the position of the child within the Symbolic as marginal/central to varying degrees. Men's femininity can show through as can women's. Men who have in their writing what Kristéva would call a 'woman's practice' would be those with an ambiguous relation between their biological sex and their self expression. Her examples are Jean Genet, James Joyce, Louis-Ferdinand Céline. Hélène Cixous would add Kleist and others.

Furthermore, Kristéva's conception of language as a process rather than a structure, with meaning constantly being created and re-created both between the signifiers (components of language) and between the signifiers and the signifieds (those things referred to by the signifiers), destroys the oppressive identities of masculine and feminine. As with Derrida's abolition of fixed meaning and identity, Kristéva's world, hidden by metaphysical thinking, is one of shifting meanings. She does not share the goal of bringing the feminine fully into existence, of defining the feminine autonomously: this remains within the boundaries of metaphysics, without challenging the notion of identity itself. She sees the feminine as existing (as do other forms of resistance to the Symbolic) in the margins, the interstices, and it must remain in this position to keep its revolutionary nature. It must exist as a constant threat to the Symbolic but not as a potential replacement for it. There can be no attempt to bind or limit its possibilities. Kristeva makes no attempt to define the feminine in such a way as to capture its 'essence': were this even possible, it is exactly what must be avoided.

Luce Irigaray, formerly a Lacanian psychoanalyst who was expelled from the *Ecole Freudienne* for her feminist challenges in her book *Speculum, de l'autre femme* (Speculum, of the Other Woman) and whose work is also inspired by Derrida's attack on logocentrism, takes a different route from Kristéva in her analysis of the feminine. Taking up Lacan's suggestion that woman does not exist, Irigaray agrees that the feminine, woman-as-concept, is always repressed into the unconscious, or foreclosed through the resolution of the Oedipus complex: that is, it remains at the level of a potentiality that cannot be developed. The notion of femininity that exists in phallogocentrism is one created in the terms of patriarchy, serving a patriarchal purpose for men who cannot even conceive of a non-phallic feminine. Irigaray believes that before a 'feminine feminine', a non-phallic feminine, can even be *thought*, women need to examine the male philosophical and psychoanalytical texts which have contributed to the construction of the 'masculine feminine', the phallic feminine, in order to locate and identify it.

This is an important aspect of her own work. Her book *Speculum, de l'autre femme* is described by Irigaray in a later collection of essays[3] as her attempt to locate this false feminine:

> . . . In *Speculum* I try to go back through the masculine Imaginary, to interpret how it has reduced us to silence, to mutism, to imitation, and I try, from there, and at the same time, to (re) find a possible space for a feminine Imaginary.[4]

Irigaray's enormous undertaking does several things simultaneously. Her examination of Plato's and Freud's theories, through deconstructive readings, is written in a way that consciously tries to maintain a distance from the phallogocentric language it attacks. Irigaray does this by refusing one, authoritative reading/approach to the text; by intimating a plurality of meanings and fully exploiting the ambiguity in language;[5] and by ignoring the rules of syntax. It is difficult to read, dense and layered, rich; her style is itself part of her resistance to the Symbolic.

Irigaray's work attacks philosophy and language aiming to show the phallogocentric bias of both our conceptual and our expressive frameworks and tools. To this end, she questions the 'categories' of philosophy and sees:

> the necessity to 'reopen' the figures of philosophy – the Idea, Substance, the Subject, transcendental subjectivity, absolute knowledge – to bring out the imprint of/to the feminine, to make them 'give back' to the feminine what they owe it. This can be done in many ways, by many paths. In fact, we must always have many.[6]

The phallogocentric desire for unity and linearity, for stable meaning, must be undermined on all fronts in many ways: one way must not dominate and eliminate others, but all are always needed.

The links that Irigaray makes between philosophy, psychoanalysis, language and women's sexuality become clear in *Ce sexe qui n'en est pas un* (This Sex Which is not One), when she talks about psychoanalysis as the discourse on sexuality but also notes how it ignores sexual differentiation in language, and ignores the existence of gendered power relations in the world when discussing feminine sexuality. And she asks what would become of psychoanalytic notions in a culture where the feminine was not repressed:

Acknowledgement of a 'specific' feminine sexuality disturbs the monopoly over values that the masculine sex has – that the father has; what meaning could the Oedipus complex have in a symbolic system other than patriarchy?[7]

The implications of this question are far-reaching for psychoanalysis, pose new questions about psychoanalysis as another, universal, patriarchal discourse, whose substance is determined by patriarchal thinking. Irigaray acknowledges that her suggestion of a 'symbolic system other than patriarchy' is only a speculation, because the exclusion of the feminine is the only reality we know thus far; the 'successful' resolution of the little girl's Oedipus complex means that her feminine difference – which exists at the level of pre-Oedipal desire and *jouissance* – has been foreclosed: 'the feminine Oedipus complex is ultimately her entry into a value system that isn't her own.'[8]

Part of this value system, its medium, which is also integral to the formulation of concepts, is language. Irigaray is among those feminist theorists for whom language is patriarchal, masculine, but has always appeared as universal, neutral – as *tout* in Lacan's terms, whereas the feminine is *pas tout*. As she replied to one woman who said that she didn't understand what 'masculine language' meant: 'Of course you don't because it's the only language there is.'[9]

It is essential to Irigaray's work to show that language is not neutral, not neuter. She believes that showing up the masculine nature of language would:

uproot phallocentrism, phallocracy, put masculinity back into language, which would leave open the possibility of a different language. Which would mean that the masculine would no longer be 'universal'. Could no longer, by itself, define, get around, delimit (the properties of) everything.[10]

Uncovering the seemingly neutral stance of language, the social sciences, philosophy, is one of the strategies employed by Irigaray to resist absorption into the male Symbolic Order, and is one way to begin to allow the feminine to exist.

The second strategy is concerned with female sexuality. Irigaray differs from Kristéva by suggesting that the feminine has certain characteristics, which *can* be described. The underlying characteristic of the feminine, for Irigaray, as for Cixous and *Psych et Po*, is multiplicity: if the basic drive of the masculine is to unify, to stabilise and rationalise, then the feminine must resist, must remain multiple and diffuse. Multiplicity begins, suggests Irigaray, at the level of women's anatomy: '. . . women don't have one sex organ. They have at least two, which can't be identified singly. Actually women have many more than that. Their sexuality, always at least double, is *plural*/multiple.'[11] Women can conceive of otherness, alterity, according to Irigaray, because they already contain otherness within them in this multiplicity. Whereas the phallic libidinal economy is described by feminists as unitary, linear and teleological and therefore unable to think alterity, the feminine is plural, circular (concentric) without goals. The expression of these libidinal economies is not restricted to sexuality and to sexual pleasure, but extends to all forms of expression, social relations and social organisations. Patriarchy is thus the expression of the masculine libidinal economy. This economy must both be understood and resisted before anything different can begin, before the feminine can exist in this phallogocentric world, and unsettle it absolutely. Irigaray re-examines women's sexuality as the possible location of the feminine. Like Kristéva, Irigaray looks to the pre-Oedipal child, in particular to the pre-Oedipal girl and to her relation to her own body and to her mother. She proposes that adult women can challenge 'Oedipisation' by homosexual and auto-erotic practice. Female sexuality is self-sufficient, suggests Irigaray, not dependent on the penis for pleasure, and while Freud had only ever considered female homosexuality on his male model, she suggests that it could be the space allowing a feminine libidinal economy to exist, undermining the phallic economy and altering more than sexual relations.

An example of Irigaray's writing in which she evokes the multiplicity of the feminine libidinal economy while writing the kind of text that challenges phallogocentric language by self-conscious distancing, is *Quand nos lèvres se parlent* (When our Lips Speak Together), an essay addressing a woman lover. The text is shot through with intimations (which is as close as we can presently get) of a different language, a language that expresses femininity in a way that our present language cannot; and a text that gives the sense that women are ill at ease in phallocentric language:

> If we go on talking the same way, if we talk to each other like men have talked to each other for centuries, as we have learned to talk, we'll miss each other. Still . . . words pass through our bodies, above our heads, to lose themselves, to lose us. Far, high. Absent from us: spoken machines, speaking machines. Enveloped in proper skins, but not ours . . .[12]

New language, new sexuality, new meanings: it is all part of the same struggle against the monopoly of the phallic. The feminine libidinal economy, unlike masculinity, is not based on possession, on trading. In female homosexuality, or auto-eroticism alone, can the feminine libidinal economy be expressed, says Irigaray:

> Exchanges that no closure, no mouth, can ever stop up. Between us, the house has no more walls, the clearing in the closure, circular language. You embrace me: the world is so big that it loses all horizons. Unsatisfied, us? Yes, if that means that we never finish. If our pleasure is to move, be moved, with no end. Always moving: the open never tires, nor becomes saturated.[13]

Writer Hélène Cixous agrees with these other thinkers that there is a feminine libidinal economy and that sexual difference is located at the level of *jouissance*. She also agrees with Irigaray that the basis of the feminine libidinal economy is multiplicity, and that any 'definition' of the feminine must always be plural and provisional: 'What strikes me is the infinite richness of their individual make up: you can't speak of *one* feminine sexuality, uniform and homogeneous, with a predictable route any more than you can speak of similar unconsciouses'.[14] Cixous believes that the feminine can be discovered and released by women themselves in their own interrogation of their sexual pleasure. The question women should be asking, according to Cixous, is not Freud's 'What does woman want?' but rather 'How do I experience my sexual pleasure?' 'What is feminine *jouissance*, where is it sited, how is it inscribed in her body, in her unconscious? And then, how can it be written?'[15] Cixous defines a feminine libidinal economy in her article *Le Sexe ou la tête* (Castration or Decapitation) as 'a regime, energies, a system of spending not necessarily carved out by culture'.[16] She holds that women can think in non-phallic ways and that women's alterity must be expressed in writing. By writing of their experience of their bodies and their sexuality, Cixous says that women can accomplish an act which will bring about a 'de-censored relation of women to their sexuality, to their being-women, giving them access to their own strength.'[17] In her theoretical texts, Cixous repeats that writing is a forceful cultural expression of women's alterity:

> I will say this: today, writing is for women. This isn't meant to incite, it simply means that: women can admit of the other . . . writing is, within me, the passage – entry, exit, duration – of the other that I am and am not, that I don't know how to be but that I feel passing . . . it is painful, it wears me out; and for men, this permeability, this non-exclusion is menacing, intolerable.[18]

Cixous describes elements that make up a feminine text in *Le Sexe ou la tête*:

> (a feminine text) is recognisable by the way it has no end (e-n-d): doesn't finish . . . The quest for origins, illustrated by Oedipus, isn't something that haunts the feminine unconscious. On the other hand, the beginning, or rather, beginnings, the way to begin, not punctually with the phallus and closing with the phallus, but starting on all sides at once, that is the inscription of the feminine . . . you can't foretell a feminine text, it can't be predicted, it doesn't know itself (isn't conscious of itself), it is therefore very troubling. You can't think it in advance, and I believe that femininity is written without anticipation: it is really the unforeseeable text.[19]

A feminine text is, for Cixous, defiance of the Symbolic, or even, as killer of the Logos, outside patriarchy's control, it is more than defiant, it is parricidal. Through writing, women gain some control. 'It is through writing as women and towards women, taking up the challenge posed by phallic discourse, that women will affirm themselves as women in a way other than in the place reserved for them in, and by, the Symbolic.'[20] A feminine text is by definition subversive, defying encoding by the Symbolic, not expressible within phallogocentrism's limits of meaning, logic and syntax, and cannot be understood in phallogocentric terms. A feminine text 'exists and will exist elsewhere, somewhere other than the territories subordinate to philosophical-theoretical domination. It won't allow itself to be thought by anyone except by destroyers of old habits, those who run along the edges, refusing to be subjugated by any authority.'[21] The feminine text will dislodge the masculine from its position as universal; and the feminine text will operate the inscription of the feminine libidinal economy into culture. Once the feminine is there, it will mean re-inscribing the masculine in a new way, toppling the binary logic of our conceptual system. Cixous holds the Derridean view on the oppressively fixed oppositions that we think with:

Man/Woman automatically means great/small, superior/inferior . . . means high or low, means Nature/History, means transformation/inertia. In fact, every theory of culture, every theory of society, the whole conglomeration of symbolic systems – everything, that is, that's spoken, everything that's organised as discourse, art, religion, the family, language, everything that seizes us, everything that acts on us – it is all ordered around hierarchical oppositions that come back to the man/woman opposition . . .[22]

The advent of the feminine means a total upheaval of the Symbolic Order, which could eventually be replaced, based on a feminine principle, allowing of difference and abolishing hierarchy, rather than on the masculine domination of the One.

While obviously legislation and material improvement to women's lives can change things for the better, no sign of truly upsetting patriarchy can exist as long as the concepts we think with, and the language we function in, remain intact. Women can begin the process of upsetting patriarchy by examining their relation to their own sexuality, to other women, to language and to writing.

The group *Psych et Po* has gone further than any other women in the attempt not merely to resist the Symbolic, but to develop a political strategy based on women's alterity. Much of their work resembles that of Hélène Cixous, who was for a long time associated with the group (but has recently distanced herself from it), yet also with that of Irigaray who is not. In the *Psych et Po* texts, some of the theoretical aspects of the re-examination of female psychosexual development are given political meaning; and similar importance is attributed to female homosexuality and to writing. Women's homosexual separatism is posited as the first step towards the Revolution of the Symbolic, while writing is given prime importance through their magazine and the publishing company.

The No.42–43 (1980) issue of *des femmes en mouvements hebdo* is devoted to the question of women's homosexuality. This is repeatedly said to be the prerequisite for removing women from the Symbolic Order into a separate female, eventually feminine, space. Female sexuality is explored through the accumulation of stories of individual sexual development, about which the authors seem to be unusually, self-consciously, aware, an awareness that follows analysis and/or their recent political awakening. One woman – all *Psych et Po* articles in the magazines were written by *une femme* (a woman) or *des femmes* (some women), avoiding public prominence of some women but also avoiding responsibility for the words and often giving misleading impressions – after writing of her own experience, says 'I feel that women will manage to free themselves from heterosexist and patriarchal structures by loving women. By becoming lesbians.' (p. 15.)

Lesbianism, a word not much used by *Psych et Po*, is one way by which women can seek to return to the intimacy of the pre-Oedipal child's relation to the mother. They claim that in female homosexuality, the Oedipus complex has been subverted by the refusal to reject the mother's body (p. 24): 'the other, "homosexual", carries within her body traces of the permanent, privileged relation to the mother's body, which she has never renounced and which she brings to bear in her homosexuality.'

Psych et Po's interpretation of the Oedipus complex is that it is experienced as a terrible loss of maternal tenderness, as rape by the father, who breaks the privileged intimacy of mother and child, the repressed traces of which remain in the body. While the homosexual woman brings out this re-found tenderness in her sexuality, a heterosexual woman is described as 'she who knows the fear, the anguish of her *jouissance*, forbidden and incessantly sought, of the repressed body.' (p.27.)

Psych et Po's advocacy of women's homosexual practice is not recommended at large, but specifically within the group itself. The inevitable *une femme* author of one tale of coming to the light illustrates the *Psych et Po* approach to the question of how to liberate women's repressed sexuality (p.28):

> I was closed up by the law and by language, walled up alive. I came back, and a woman's word, flying in the face of language, a voice with the register of a buried body . . . made its way up to my unlistening ear . . . I was no longer amnesiac, forgetting my own *jouissance* . . . And this encounter with women for whom women have stayed love object. By their desire, to begin again from the wellbeing of a primary rapport, a primary body, remake our history, differently . . . Understand that this *jouissance*, this other economy, is what constitutes the women's movement.

All the elements of a *Psych et Po* reading are present in this extract: women's repression by the Symbolic Order represented by law and language; a different libidinal economy; the first bodily contact with the mother; the repression of feminine *jouissance* in heterosexuality, and the liberation of this different economy in homosexuality.

Psych et Po's approach to women's alterity in general and to female homosexuality as a strategy of difference, clearly locates themselves as the (only) space for the feminine challenge to the Symbolic Order. If female homosexuality is the first step for women's 'real' liberation, it is within the MLF *marque déposée* alone that this is possible.[23] While Irigaray and Cixous, positively and politically motivated, treated the feminine as a discursive and sexual potential, to be worked towards, *Psych et Po* – who claim to have gone beyond patriarchy – believe that they incarnate the feminine: indeed, they call the group (now, the MLF), a 'homosexed movement to bring the feminine into existence.' They are the sole crusaders of the feminine, at the forefront of the Revolution of the Symbolic.

The feminist theoretical enterprise is nothing less than the attempt to understand the world and women's place in it in a way that accounts for gender difference at all levels; and, denying that any philosophy is disinterested, feminist critiques of the entire edifice of Western philosophical thought are openly politically implicated in what they say. The disruption foreseen by the advent of the feminine creates a potential disturbance of patriarchy/phallogocentrism that is exciting. As Hélène Cixous says:

> The questioning of this solidarity between logocentrism and phallocentrism has become urgent enough – revealing what has been done to women, how the feminine has been buried – to

threaten the masculine edifice that pretends it is natural-eternal;
by bringing out, on femininity's side, questions and hypotheses
that are necessarily destructive of the bastion of authority. What
would happen to the logocentrism of great philosophical systems,
to order in the world in general, if the cornerstone, the
foundation stone of their church crumbled?[24]

By assigning certain attributes to phallogocentrism and to the feminine, defined as the opposite of phallogocentrism, the as yet unknown woman can begin to be discovered. The pessimism – or
political quietism – of the male philosophers, the sense that patriarchy, as social organisation and as discourse, is inevitable, is contested.
The political goals of feminism, diverse as they are, have led theorists
to push forward, to look forward to a feminist, feminine practice that
deranges and disorders phallogocentrism. While Derrida's work
fuels the feminist rejection of the system that represses difference,
casting off the notion that because this is the way things have always
been so far, this is the way they will always be, naturally and
unchangeably, the feminist thinkers have added a Utopian edge to
their thought. For if Derrida, Foucault, Lacan and others leave room
for difference to be thought, and thought differently, the envisaging
of this difference heralds an unrepressed future that remains specula-
tive. Only feminists seem to think that this perfectly unoppressive
world is possible.

Lacan's work has provided the basis for the whole theoretical
framework of *Psych et Po*, who accept that social interaction takes
place in the registers of the Imaginary and the Symbolic; the positing
of a repressed feminine libidinal economy and a feminine jouissance
outside the phallic; the radical otherness of woman. *Psych et Po's*
strategy for the liberation of women (of woman?) is therefore
undertaken as a response to the Lacanian schema, not challenging its
organisation, only its limitations. *Psych et Po* have developed
strategies that they believe will provide ways to nurture the newly-
born feminine (born in the group), to resist the dictatorship of the
Symbolic and to encourage a space in which that feminine can
develop. Writing, and sexual separatism are seen as ways to resist the
repressive, reductive tendencies of phallogocentrism with the ultimate goal of using these resistances to bring about a world of
heterogeneous meaning and feminine multiplicity.

The overwhelming importance of women's alterity for French

feminists is further sustained by the male philosophers' attack on the notion of the 'subject'. The erosion of Cartesian identity – the integrated, coherent, intentional subject – by Derrida, Foucault and Lacan has renewed attention to *all* forms of otherness. If the validity of the thinking, self-conscious subject, the *cogito*, is undermined, then the invalidity of otherness is equally undermined. The hierarchy between the two, giving phallogocentrism privilege at the expense of otherness, and defining otherness in terms of phallogocentric, metaphysical (and therefore illusory) identity, will be unbalanced, and otherness as a valid, autonomously-defined concept could be made possible. Feminism has benefited from, and participated in, an epistemological upheaval that has undone notions of the integrity of identity and the authority of meaning, opening up new areas as yet unthought, among which is the concept of the feminine.

At the base of all otherness and of feminine alterity in particular, is multiplicity. For some, multiplicity begins at the level of women's anatomy, libido and *jouissance*, expressed in certain styles of writing and in women's homosexuality. On a philosophical level, it means resistance to organisation, to the one-ness, the unicity, of phallogo-centrism, challenging the values and concepts of masculine discourse from a position marginal to that discourse, distanced from it (or, for *Psych et Po*, optimistically outside it?); on a political level, multiplic-ity means resistance to organisation and hierarchy of structure, commitment to a plurality of voice and style and structure.[25] The insistence on multiplicity, whether as an ontological premise or more simply as rejection of what has been defined as male metaphysics or male political practice and organisation, is shared by all French feminists, whatever their particular orientations. The divergent understandings of the meaning of multiplicity is itself an example of multiplicity.

To this concept of the feminine, I want to adopt a positive yet critical perspective. I am by no means alone in my criticisms of the feminine: it has been rejected outright by French radical feminists and by other materialist feminists as based in an essentialism, an ahistorical essence, which can only play against women in a political struggle. Yet the arguments in favour of a discursive revolution as an integral part of a political struggle are convincing. It seems as though interesting and complex ideas have been collapsed together and need to be sorted out.

Sexual difference does indeed seem to me to be the basis of different life experience and at the root of women's oppression in cultural as well as material terms (with so-called masculine values prized at the expense of 'feminine' values and characteristics). But I am not convinced by the revolutionary programme to bring the feminine into existence, nor by some of the undiscussed assumptions of the concept itself, and I am concerned by its political implications.

The starting point of the definition of masculine and feminine libidinal economies is said to be women's anatomy (for Irigaray), and *jouissance* in its simplest meaning of the difference between the masculine and feminine experience of sexual pleasure. This is the starting point because it is something that escapes discourse, unmediated by language and society. Using a model of male sexuality and its opposite, masculine and feminine characteristics are derived from bodily experience: for instance, linearity is said to be masculine, ex-centricity, looking outwards and in a circular fashion, is said to be feminine; goal orientation would be masculine and lack of goal orientation feminine, and so on. There are, for me, a number of problems in this. The suggestion of beginning all things with bodily experience and anatomy is troublesome. It may be the way to incorporate the body into theory and overcome the body/spirit metaphysical duality, but if we examine *jouissance* as the basis of difference organisations of energy that precede and determine our social existences, it nonetheless means that we have, in some sense, to know *jouissance*; to recognise and express our experience. And knowledge, consciousness of something, recognition, implies distancing, implies language and implicates our social beings. We cannot know things except through language and through the concepts we possess. Our knowledge of *jouissance*, then, either remains inadequate and outside our comprehension, or reduced from its original radical otherness, because that otherness can't be expressed in our only ways of knowing and expressing. And if it remains outside, escaping distortion and circumscription by metaphysical masculinity, remaining at the level of bodily experience, or if it is reduced to something our minds can apprehend, then how can its disruptive potential ever be released? How can it ever mean more? Is its significance precisely in confronting the knowledge that there is something that we cannot know? But then, if masculine *jouissance* is the only kind that can be described and apprehended in language, in patriarchy, then the feminine *can* be described, but only as the opposite of the masculine. But this leaves us within metaphysics, still thinking in terms of opposites instead of differences. And can we be so sure that *jouissance* escapes contamination by society? Does this reliance on sexual pleasure not eliminate the social too insistently, ignoring the person and what the person brings, what other 'baggage', to sexual pleasure? Or if *jouissance* is supposed to mean something existing within us and determining our behaviour and experience without reference to actual physical experience, then where do we start to try to define libidinal economy at all?

I would also question the way all traits are said to be derived from masculine and feminine. Can we really draw conclusions from difference of bodily experience and extend them into generally identifying features of 'masculinity' and 'femininity'? What becomes labelled as one or the other? Who decides? Tiresias? Is it legitimate to seek a new identity that relies so heavily on the body, rather than incorporating the body with other elements that could equally be said to contribute to who and what we are? Having contested the definition of women's behaviour and nature that Freud set out and the way he linked 'female' sexual passivity with women's social behaviour, feminists eager to explore a new feminine should be wary of making exaggerated leaps into definitions. The concept of the feminine could merely replace one conceptual prison by another. The Feminine, as 'transcendental signified', could easily become the factor that makes sense of the world, in terms of which everything can and must be explained. This is what I think has happened with *Psych et Po*. Apart from Kristéva, who attacks the notion of identity as such, many feminists do seem to call for a certain extent of definition for the feminine, be it provisional, plural, diffuse and vague.

Psych et Po seem to have embarked on the first stage of discovering the feminine, which for them, involves reversing the hierarchy of values dominant in patriarchy: reversal precedes elimination of the opposites altogether. All things suggested to be feminine – lack of closure, giving, opening and so on – are paid renewed attention and ascribed with new value. However, is this reversal the first phase of a disruption, or will it merely paralyse? How can the next phase be reached? The paradox for *Psych et Po* is that seeking a way for the feminine to provide a basis for action means that a minimum of definition is vital, and then the feminine itself becomes, to a certain extent, fixed and limited.

Psych et Po's firm belief in the feminine tells us about their political actions and attitudes to feminism and to women. Belief in their project as the only valid revolution for women means that all other feminist approaches are denied any value: women whose struggle is in the context of the Symbolic Order, who want to change laws but not language, are, in *Psych et Po's* terms probably wasting their time. Women must place themselves outside patriarchy – as if this were possible – withdraw from institutions, remove themselves from men, understand masculinity and eliminate it from their heads. It clearly means a very particular kind of existence and an increased inability of women in the group to relate to those not in the group, or to have any respect for what other women are trying to do. On top of this, *Psych et Po's* ideas are elitist as well as exclusive. For them, the 'true' feminine, 'real' women, are only now beginning to exist (inside the group), and women's past lives are only useful as material for analysis: the 'before' in a 'before and after' story. We are all phallic women; none of our experience as women is as 'real', feminine, women, and *Psych et Po* are apparently the only ones who have even a glimmer about what this could be. They do not worry about women for whom Lacanian theory is impossible to understand (or who have never heard of Lacan); about those whose production is reproduction; about those whose lives remain tied to men's; who have not been able or willing to make the same radical choices. The work to bring the feminine into existence leads to a practice that is profoundly anti-women.

'Bringing the feminine into existence' is itself problematic. Working from the assumption that there is this buried, undiscovered feminine libidinal economy that can and must be allowed to come to life through psychoanalytic exploration, *Psych et Po* propose a return to the mother's body and the rejection of the Father, to be achieved via their various strategies. The ultimate goal seems to be the creation of feminine unconscious structures through work on the unconscious. They are treading the precarious path of suggesting a conscious agenda for the construction of a new, authentic, feminine unconscious that could then find expression. Yet would this feminine unconscious be any less artificial than the masculine, imposed unconscious is said to be? Would a feminine version of the feminine be any more real than the phallic feminine? How would real feminine women function in the rest of the patriarchal world? Who would say when the feminine feminine had been reached?

The whole idea of a 'real' feminine implies a state prior to social existence, which is said to be distorted through unconscious as well as through social, conscious, procedures. There is assumed to be a true, undistorted female sexuality, libidinal economy, waiting for the right time to emerge, like a butterfly. Is this not simply a romantic notion, somewhat like the idea of the noble savage? Can a latent state of femininity be consciously brought out of its latency? The idea is not only in conflict with Lacan and Derrida (Lacan may agree with the undiscovered feminine, but cheerfully believes it will stay undiscovered; Derrida has no use for notions such as 'true' or 'identity' anyway), but more importantly, it is in conflict with feminist practice. It is impossible to say that feminine difference can be divorced from the historical use made of that notion: and feminine difference has always been used to oppress women, just as other kinds of difference (racial, linguistic, class, etc.) have been used to justify oppression.

It would be unfortunate to dismiss the notion of feminine difference altogether, and wrong to deny that there is a difference in men and women's life experience and perceptions. However, even this sentence indicates how ambiguous the relationship of feminine difference to women is. On the one hand, the feminine appears as a discursive challenge to meaning and identity, freedom from the restrictions of 'men must be "masculine" and women "feminine" ' in the stereotypical way that we know. On the other hand, women's bodies provide the site for the will to find a new feminine: in feminist politics, the feminine, with its disruptive power, belongs to women. But once the feminine becomes the prerogative of women, all the problems wrapped up in fixing identity and developing strategy from that identity begin, and close in on, dispel, the challenge.

For those feminists who dream of a future where the feminine exists, and where difference is no longer repressed, there are still problems. Derrida, in his destruction of confidence in Western Judeo-Christian metaphysics, warns that this destruction of confidence is as far as we can go: self-conscious distancing is our limit. To imagine going beyond this is to imagine a world in which heterogeneity of meaning and inconclusivity of meaning can exist. As an underlying principle of a Utopian society where nobody oppresses anybody else, where no one can dictate what is right and true, where meanings abound and organisation becomes egalitarian, this heterogeneity, this multiplicity sounds attractive. However the reality of a world that is provisional in meanings, where logic is denigrated as a

101

mode of thought, where all interpretations are valid and values are upset but not replaced, would be impossible. Reminding us that the world we live in and the codes we live by are neither natural nor innocent is one thing, and can be used to help us understand the world as we know it, but can hardly provide us with a new world that can grow out of this one. In the understandable eagerness to topple masculine meanings from their pedestal, feminists have failed to imagine how each woman and man could situate themselves in this new world, how new conceptual frameworks could be developed, how values and priorities decided and how boundaries set: for all these things must exist, if differently.

The danger of difference is that it can lead to a political and theoretical impasse, to a political 'ghetto' shared by the happy few and divorced from the rest, using language and ideas in such a specific way that no one else can understand what they are doing, and ignoring the material conditions of women's lives. The danger of rejecting difference lies in ignoring the way patriarchy enters us and forgetting the way in which different levels of oppression affect and involve each other.

As is clear from these last pages, I have no answers to offer and no positions to set out, just questions. I would finally ask, though, whether we have really reached the point where women can propose strategies on the basis of assuming that the answers have been found when the questions themselves have not yet been adequately formulated.

CHAPTER 6

A different politics

One of the questions most vital to examine is, I think, what the implications of difference are for feminist politics. If the women's movement believes strongly that theory and practice go hand in hand, and that the production of theory is tied to women's lives and strategies for change, then any discussion of feminist theoretical work must involve discussion of political activity, and the issues raised in Chapter 5 must be linked to political reality in France. This chapter, then, asks what the strategic implications of feminine difference are for feminist politics; and what 'multiplicity' means in terms of structure and activity for the MLF.

The focus will be on the fragile political space that feminism occupies in mainstream French political life. *Psych et Po* may aim for a politics of difference, but other feminists reject this in favour of something that seems more simple but is, I believe, far more complex and difficult: a different politics. What happens when feminists attempt to create a politics that both expresses a different idea about political theory, and a desire for procedures that are different from those which already exist in the political arena, but which at the same time operates within the boundaries of that arena? It is easy to speculate: but I have tried to anchor my speculations in the experience of feminists in two political parties, those which – of the major parties – seem the most accessible to feminism for ideological and practical reasons. These are the Socialist Party (PS) and the more marginal, but still influential, *Parti Socialiste Unifié* (PSU).

Feminism seems to be in clear contradiction to the imperatives of party politics. Fundamental to feminism is its multiplicity of approach, diversity of formation, rejection of hierarchy, its revision of the meaning of politics and open-endedness of analysis. Electoral politics, however, require a political programme and platform. Politicians have to demonstrate that they have a particular vision of the society they would like to see and are capable of developing sets of measures, adopting positions and working out viable strategies in order to realise that society and make it work. The substance of political statements must be expressed in a particular kind of rhetoric, in such a way that the public will be convinced enough to vote for that particular party. The direct goal of the party is to gain power, and once gained, to keep it, and this goal largely determines both the discourse and the strategy of the party.

Between feminism and competitive party politics – which forms the institutional framework of democratic societies – there seems to be a gulf over attitudes to power, to means and ends, to the meaning of politics and to the way in which political life is conducted. Even so, feminist groups are obliged to confront the question of their relation to political institutions, whether they end up by totally rejecting, or pragmatically accepting, the rules that make up the political game. When the rather vague feminist ideal of an oppression-free society is contrasted with the needs of a political party, which has to formulate its ideals in terms of concrete, realisable goals and administrative practicalities, it is evident that feminist insertion into party politics will be problematic.

In 1970, all the women who called themselves part of the MLF rejected both the notion of politics that was current, and the procedures that dominated party politics. Politics and politicians had developed a bad reputation: people thought of politics as competition between parties, government decisions, electoral strategy, that had little or nothing to do with anyone except politicians. Those who knew the rules played the game, while everyone else looked on, more or less passively. The game itself was discredited, while the players were thought of as ambitious, self-serving and manipulative. And in this disappointing public spectacle, women had a specific complaint: the political system did not represent women.

It is true to say that women have remained largely excluded from both access to political power and from decision-making processes, and have also been generally passive as citizens (because they are not represented?). Even when women form a significant percentage of membership of one party or another, their representation in the party's decision-making bodies remains very low.[1] Numbers of women candidates for election are also extremely low, although efforts are being made to increase them.

Political scientists, researchers and feminists have tried to find out why women have been so absent from the traditional political front.[2] Reasons include social expectations of boys and girls, 'choices' made at school, the way that the classic *cursus politicus* – which takes the nation's youthful elite from the top French *lycées* through specialised training at the *grandes écoles* to the prestigious *Ecole Nationale d'Administration* (ENA)[3] conflicts with the image of what women should be aiming for in French society.

There is also the fact that women in France were given the vote only in 1944, written into the French Constitution of 1946. This had several effects. First, the lack of access to political power and influence[4] through full citizenship meant that women have always sought other paths for action, such as social work, voluntary associations or influence in the family. The division of women's work in the so-called private sphere and men's in the public, perpetuated the image of women not belonging to politics; and once women dominated in one field or another (for instance primary school teaching, which was a highly political profession in the time of the Third Republic), it lost its political image and overtones.

A report on women in French society commissioned by the new Ministry for Women's Rights in 1981[5] still commented on women's absence from politics, and lack of integration into the political system. Some researchers found that women's political awareness depended mainly on whether or not they exercised, or had ever exercised, a profession; another suggested that the strong influence of religion over some women played an important role in determining political interest and integration. The women who were least involved in things political were found to be those workers' wives who were practising Catholics and who had never worked outside the home themselves. A third inquiry suggested that for women to identify with the political system, the nature of politics would have to change, and the disparity between what was perceived as political and the social image of women would have to be overcome.

A principal feminist concern has been to try to find ways to 'translate women's experience into political projects', that is, to try to overcome this disparity and combine women's reality with political reality. This has meant that the MLF has addressed questions of electoral participation and of participation in party politics as well as question of its own autonomous forms of organisation since the early 1970s. Some women felt that, as women formed 53 per cent of the population in France, it was important for women to vote, to influence legislation, to seek positions of leadership themselves and be instrumental in changing not only what can be discussed in political terms but also the ways in which political life is conducted. Others have rejected any form of participation in politics at all. For much of the decade of the 1970s, women called for abstention on the grounds that women were not merely ignored by political parties, but that these parties tacitly or actively perpetuated women's oppression, and could therefore not be supported. Before the March 1978 elections for a new parliament, several women from non-aligned feminist groups explained their refusal to vote in a letter to *Le Monde* (23 December, 1977). They would not vote, they said:

... because we believe that the positions held by the Left, as well as the Right, are inadequate where the 'women's question' is concerned. Because the struggle against the roots of women's oppression, the patriarchal family, isn't taken into account by any existing political party. Because we think that their positions are inadequate precisely because, with male leaders, it is in these parties' interest to maintain our oppression . . . (We won't vote) also and above all, because for us, feminism isn't something on the side that can be added to a programme or dealt with separately, but constitutes the basis of our politics. Which woman would want to support parties that share in oppressing her?

Psych et Po's refusal to vote stemmed from their placing women in a political and theoretical dimension beyond patriarchy. A poster of theirs was reproduced before the 1978 legislative elections *(des femmes en mouvements mensuelle* No. 3, 1978), saying:

in a capitalist, imperialist, patriarchal state
to vote is to reinforce the power system.
We will not give our voices
to those who make laws, who make the law
we are not representable

we struggle together outside the law
to overthrow capitalist, imperialist
patriarchal power
so that women and all oppressed people
together, can think, speak, act.

Given their particular approach, it was predictable that *Psych et Po* would not vote. Fears that non-participation would leave the MLF in a political and cultural 'ghetto' did not bother *Psych et Po*, who felt that the very term 'ghetto' was a male-centred perspective used by men to counter their fear of the power of the feminine, and was irrelevant to the creation of a new feminine space from which to speak. Other women, however, were unhappy with the silence of non-participation and chose the risks involved in participation – the dangers of co-option and distortion – rather than remaining silent. The conflict must be faced that by actively participating in political life, for instance, in standing for election, women agree to play the game that perpetuates their own oppression; but it is also the chance for a woman to speak out and to help change that game from inside.

The difficulties of women, particularly feminists, in political parties are compounded by the attitudes of the men in those parties. Feminists who choose involvement with party politics will choose parties on the Left; parties on the Right, such as the Gaullist party of Jacques Chirac would never agree that women are oppressed in the first place and encourage women to put their role as wife and mother first (as their natural place). Right-wing parties put forward a view of the French nation as unified, each section of society contributing its own special talents. Left-wing parties do not subscribe to this myth and have a particular notion of oppression, but this doesn't mean that men in the Left accept that women are subjected to a specific oppression, and that they themselves can be accused of being oppressive. The increasing disaffection of women with their male comrades in far-Left revolutionary organisations has already been mentioned as one of the factors that helped women see the need to organise autonomously. Women who joined the PCF, the PS and the PSU shared the cynicism of their 'revolutionary' sisters, but were equally, or more, determined to make their 'double militancy' work.

This determination came up against endless obstacles, most obviously in the PCF, which is not known for its tolerance of those who disagree with party line. When there is dissent, especially in

107

public, the dissenters find themselves excluded from the party. Women in the party were expected to agree with party line, particularly as the PCF claimed to be 'the party of women's liberation'. In the same way as *Psych et Po* claimed to be the only real group to understand women's oppression, the only one to be doing anything about it, the PCF claimed that only through the party would women ever be liberated. According to the PCF, feminists failed to understand the nature of oppression:

Unlike feminists, who place themselves entirely within the dominant ideology, we do not believe that inequality results from a collective male plot . . . by believing this, feminists are not only mistaken, but they are unaffected by changes around them and they deny any possibility of modifying anything . . .

---

said the PCF in 1978.[6]

That same year, a collective of feminists in the PCF formed and wrote an article called *Le Parti mis à nu par ses femmes* (the party exposed by its women), criticising party practice. They offered it to the PCF newspaper *L'Humanité*, which refused to publish it. They then offered it to *Le Monde* which did print it, on June 12, 1978. The women were promptly accused of washing dirty linen in public and betraying the party. As the dissident women noted bitterly in their magazine *Elles voient rouge* (No.0, 1979), 'when communist women dare express anything other than a blissful sense of well-being in the party, the party won't publish what they say.' It was made impossible for feminist communists to stay in the party if they had a different analysis of women's 'condition' from the analysis put forward by the party: anything different was either ignored or rejected out of hand.

Non-communist feminists were luckier in belonging to parties with a less monolithic structure: parties that could welcome diversity as part of their policy. The PS and the PSU are both theoretically composed of currents with different political analyses, and both espouse feminist ideals. The hopes that feminists could find a space of their own within a party, speak and be heard in the party, avoid co-option and yet play a significant part in the political process, have therefore frequently been pinned onto either the PS or the PSU.

Inside the Socialist Party, feminists felt that the best way to be heard in the party was to form a separate current, in the same way that there was a Mitterrand current, a current led by Pierre Mauroy

(Mitterrand's first Prime Minister, from 1981–summer 1984), another, Marxist, current led by Jean-Pierre Chevènement (now Education Minister), and so on. To form a current in the PS, the founders have to produce a *motion* (a proposal) which would then be discussed at the different levels of party hierarchy – Section, Federation and National Congress. At the National Congress, there would be a vote, and if the founders won more than 5 per cent of the party membership's vote, the current's delegates would be included in party decision-making at national level.

The idea of a feminist current in the PS met with hostility from both men and women in the party. Yvette Roudy, now Minister for Women's Rights, was one who opposed the current. She said (*Le Matin*, 8 June 1978):

> Forming a current in the PS means more than putting one's ideas on the agenda. It isn't simply expressing the needs of one group, as some people may think. It is completely different. Whoever talks about a current in the PS is talking about a project for society, complete with a strategy for gaining power, and a particular perspective on the question of the transition to this society. Question: what future is there in an autonomous feminist project, built by women's words and not in the context of the socialist project, unless it is to divide our women's struggle and the workers' struggle, and thereby weaken us on both fronts?

This attitude to the feminist current was held by many PS members and it soon became clear that participation in the new current might cost women their chance of a career in the PS. Some of the original founders decided to withdraw from their part in the feminist proposal and continue their fight for women within an existent current. The others, who went ahead, accepted this withdrawal as potentially useful to women and understood and accepted the desire for a political career and its importance. They did not dissociate from these other women in the name of feminist integrity, and believed that all feminists in the party could help each other.

The proposal was drawn up and presented to the PS at its National Congress in Metz in 1979.

> Odette Brun: Our proposal was completely original in that we put forward a project for society taking women's oppression as

our starting point – no one had done this before us and no one has done it since. Women in the PS now add chapters on women to their current's proposal and try to push for things that will help women's lives and so on, but what we had was a global political analysis and project.

Marie-Claude Ripert: Others hitched the feminist wagon to the rest, but we didn't. The PS says that capitalism is the main oppression. We say that the main oppression is the oppression that men exercise over women, that it is this oppression that structures societies and it was this oppression that we wanted to fight. And only feminism could offer a politics on this basis.

CD: Well why did you choose the PS?

Marie-Claude Ripert: Only the PS had structures allowing us to do this – you couldn't change things in the PC and the MRG (*Mouvements des Radicaux de Gauche*) just wasn't significant enough – the PS was the only party of the Left that we could work in.

CD: Not the PSU?

Françoise Grux: We wanted power. There has been a long debate over whether we should stay marginal and criticise power or whether we should try to get to the point where we can share in this power.

Lucette Saskis: We also wanted to change the PS, transform the way it functioned, try to organise a current differently, along more collective lines –

Marie-Claude Ripert: Yes, our proposal was the only one without someone's name at the top – we wanted to get away from the idea of leaders.

Andrée Cabada: And that bothered them a lot – they needed to have a spokesperson.

Edith Lhuillier: The problem was really one about what relation we should have to institutions. I think that until us, there had been two types of strategy. The MLF, at that time anyway, refused to pose the question of institutions, and others, such as Yvette Roudy, had a strategy of entryism – play the game and gain power in the ways decided by the PS. What we did was original in relation to these two strategies. We were all involved in the women's movement (cries of disagreement) and what we wanted was to find a meeting point between the women's movement and the labour movement, led by men . . . .

Marie-Claude Ripert: Just to show you that that's Edith's version
of the current's aims, I, for one, wasn't the slightest bit interested
in the labour movement. The PS isn't the same thing as the labour
movement. For me, the PS was a platform, a good chance for
feminism to be heard. The problems of males between themselves
wasn't my problem. And when the idea of a women's current was
going around, I thought, yes, *that's* what I'm interested in, and
that's what has kept me in the party and why I'm still there
although most of the others here have left. I don't think that
women should stay outside institutions – you can attack citadels
from outside but its easier when there are people inside too – look
at the Trojan wars – you see it's a very old strategy . . .
Odette Brun: A number of us became feminists after joining the
PS – some before – others came to the PS *because* of the women's
current – we all had different experiences, a different past, which
complemented each other.
Françoise Grux: To go back to Marie-Claude's ideas. I think that
the PS was the only political party which could structurally allow
women to use men's arguments (egalitarianism for instance) to
insert their own ideas –
Marie-Claude Ripert: It was the only opening, the only breach in
the male political system. On the Right there was none of this
egalitarian talk. The PS was the only place where women could
begin to open the door.
Lucette Soskis: I didn't come to the PS out of feminism. I've
always been interested in women's issues but on an individual
level. I signed the Manifesto of the 343 but on an individual basis,
not as a party member. I used to be in the PCF and already came
up against the 'women's question' because I didn't like their
negative stand on contraception. But at that time women weren't
organised in the PCF. Women complained to each other in
corners . . . I left the PC for political reasons, I was outraged that
the party was against contraception, including the women leaders.
And then when the PS was formed (1971), many former PCF
members joined and women's issues were quickly raised. One of
the reasons that the first attempt at a women's current didn't
work (the *courant 3*) was that women had their first allegiance to
an established current and only second to their feminism and it
didn't work. In the *courant G* we put our feminism first to the
point that wherever we had women in the current in positions of

111

responsibility in the PS – at local or regional level – who had to
vote on issues, we hardly ever actually voted because we felt that
the other currents were all the same and over the questions we
were concerned with, neither the CERES or the Rocardian
current had anything to offer . . .

Anne le Gall: I'd also like to explain why I joined the PS. Public
life has always demanded my attention and I've always been
active. For me, the main event was the colonial wars of the 1950s,
and the only party that spoke out against them, courageously and
in isolation, was the PC – but I couldn't join because of its links
to the Soviet Union and so I didn't actually join any party for
years. I joined the PS because it seemed at least to be moving
towards fighting for a change of political regime in France, and I
joined to *change* the party. I didn't join the Gaullist party because
the PS was at least against oppression while the RPR is based on
Christian patriarchal ideas, which is not the same thing at all, and
even though the PS ideology which states that it's against
oppression often remains skin-deep or on paper only, it is at least
a start.

But what remained for me the most important, permanent
question of all, was the women's question. When I joined, there
were two major PS currents, the CERES and Mitterrand (cries of
'and Poperen' – whose current wanted links with the PCF).
Anyway I was active in PS women's groups, which had the idea
that all the women in the different currents in the PS should get
together to push forward the discussion about women in the
party. I think it was inevitable, necessary, that we had to found a
women's current. It was a scandalous idea then, even within the
women's groups – we even debated over whether we should call it
feminist. Fifteen years ago feminism was seen as a deviation from
socialism. The women's groups were called groups for *Action
Féminine* (women's actions), not feminist. We started thinking
about a feminist current after the Party Congress at Nantes in
1977 and we managed to call it feminist and then we added
'autonomous' . . .

The proposal was an indictment of both PS analysis of women's role
in capitalist society and of party treatment of women in its ranks. It
suggests new directions for thinking out party positions, and calls for
the party to 'modify its political analysis, rethink its strategy and its

mode of operation, and accept that it must confront the most basic of conflicts: the relationship between women and men.'

The Congress gave only 1 per cent of its delegates' votes to the proposal and the current could therefore not become a fully-fledged, integrated current which could be considered a full partner in the party at national level. The current did however win representatives in two Federations (organised at regional level) and was well-represented at local level. This was seen as a modest success, and a victory for feminism, but it was also noted that as party hierarchy ascended, representatives of the feminist current disappeared; and while feminists were acknowledged as active militants at local level, they were excluded at national level from any contribution to the elaboration of the PS programme, the *Projet Socialiste* (the socialist project).

The women of the feminist current put out their own magazine, *Mignonnes, allons voir sous la rose*[7], in which they set out their own ideas, and discussed their own role in the PS and their criticisms of the party. They objected to the socialist project on several grounds: that the party's adoption of feminism was purely formal and no real attention was paid to analysing women's status in society; that while in the first section of the project the party claims to recognise the need to learn from the women's movement, there is no follow-up of this intention later; there is no attempt to discuss the relation of women to the economy, and no mention that there could be a specific relation to questions of class at all. Knowing full well that the PS membership would approve the socialist project as the sum of the contributions of the different currents, the feminist current still voted against it as a voice of protest. They also knew that their constant criticism of the party was gaining them the reputation of being either irritating or hysterical, but felt that to retreat from their feminist positions would ultimately hurt the socialist party as a whole. They were not undaunted but still determined to find a way of staying in the PS and exerting critical pressure on party policy and on the party apparatus, so that party leaders would be forced to listen to them and take feminism into account in the formulation of the party programme.

These efforts were complicated by the 1981 presidential elections. Elections are a time when party members draw together, and where a united front facing the public is essential with all members solidly behind their candidate. The candidate of the PS was François Mitterrand. There was, however, another candidate who stood explicitly as

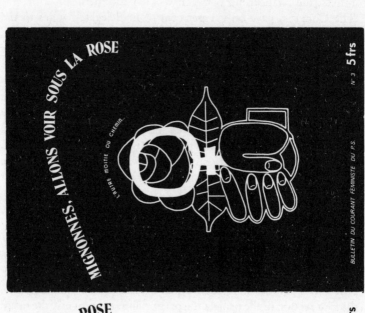

Feminism refreshes socialism

a feminist, but was the national secretary of a different party, the PSU – Parti Socialiste Unifié, a small party to the left of the PS, with strong emphasis on self-management, on theory and internal debate. This was Huguette Bouchardeau, of whom the socialist feminist current wrote (*Mignonnes* . . . No.5, 1981):

> We know her, we've met her from things we do in the women's movement: we've worked with her. As feminists, we know that we share the same ideas. There isn't one line of her political statement that we disagree with.

Feminists in the PS wanted badly to support Bouchardeau, but felt obliged to vote for Mitterrand as their own party candidate. In France, the President is elected in a two-ballot system, with the second ballot as a run-off between the two candidates who received the highest number of votes in the first round. The strong candidates in 1981 were Mitterrand, the then President Valéry Giscard d'Estaing and the second candidate of the Right, the Gaullist Jacques Chirac. The Communist leader Georges Marchais was never really a contender for a place in the second ballot. The danger for the Left was that the second ballot could easily have been between the two candidates of the Right. To ensure a Left presence in the second ballot, Mitterrand needed the support of the smaller parties of the Left (the PSU, the ecologists, the Trotskyists), as well as some PC votes and the socialist vote. Many women who wanted to vote for Bouchardeau ended by voting for Mitterrand for practical rather than ideological reasons, in a tactical vote that paid off because he won. The feminist current thought that a compromise position might be possible and that Mitterrand could negotiate a platform of action for women with them and with Bouchardeau, which could be presented as Mitterrand's positions on women at the second ballot. Mitterrand, however, chose to adopt the programme for women proposed by the association *Choisir*, while Bouchardeau adopted the proposal of the PS feminists in the first ballot. She received a negligible percentage of the total vote, less even then ultra-right-wing Marie-France Garaud and ultra-left Arlette Laguiller. The feminist vote in the PS was split between the two candidates Mitterrand and Bouchardeau. Most prominent PS women voted for Mitterrand, but others – including Edith Lhuillier, one of the founders of the feminist current, and also including women from other currents in the party – felt that they

were obliged to vote for a candidate who represented their views and
positions as closely as Bouchardeau.

Anne: The current's problems were not only created by those
outside, but came, primarily, from tensions among the women
themselves. I think we should talk about how we dealt with each
other inside the current, as it wasn't at all monolithic . . .
Françoise: And became less and less so. We split off in all
directions, to the point that some of us are still in the party and
others are not.
Anne: The trouble with *Mignonnes* was that it never reflected the
atmosphere between us. It was very tense (murmurs of
agreement).
CD: What did you split up about?
Anne: About whether it should be a women-only current, for a
start.
Odette: The PS is a mixed party, and men could vote for our
current as in fact many did.
Lucette: A current is formed by the people who vote for it and
even if it had only been women who presented the proposal, we
couldn't have stopped men voting for it and belonging to the
current.
Edith: If you're going to play the institutional game, in a sense
you are obliged to play it properly (disagreement).
Andrée: When we put forward our first proposal the question of
being a women-only current never came up. We collected all the
votes we could and we didn't exclude men. We got 5 per cent in
two Federations . . .
Lucette: We got 5 per cent in those Federations where we were
very active and where there were lots of us.
Marie-Claude: And the men in the Federations couldn't abide us
– in my Federation our votes were crucial because they upset the
balance of power between the currents – we held the power
balance and the men felt the danger, said we were a destabilising
influence – like witches – and we were thrown out of the party
(and later re-instated). They couldn't bear feminists, especially
women who lived without men. The 3 per cent we had in our
Federation disturbed the balance, disturbed the men because they
knew we wouldn't compromise, we wouldn't give in.
Lucette: Neither would we in our Federation.

Solange: We were talking about being women-only or not . . .
Françoise: We really fought over this one, you have to admit.
Lucette: It was a question of principle.
Marie-Claude Françoise: No it wasn't, it was a question of
political analysis.
Andrée: I voted against it being a women-only current because it
would have been suicidal for us.
Edith: If you were so certain that you wanted a women-only
group, why did't you go to the MLF?
Françoise: I can tell you very clearly: I did go to MLF meetings,
believe me I went, to *Psych et Po* meetings and the rest, but I
never found a political analysis that suited me. Every meeting I
went to, I ended up thinking this is awful . . . I didn't share their
analysis, didn't find a style of organisation that I agreed with.
Marie-Claude: We weren't content to stay outside institutions – I
thought that to do that was a strategic error. I didn't like the
MLF's marginality.
Anne: But the two things don't exclude each other, you can be
both in the MLF and within party structures, theoretically
anyway – what we haven't found is the space we can occupy.

Huguette Bouchardeau, too, is concerned to find a potential space for
feminists to occupy. In her book *Un Coin dans leur monde*[8] (A
Corner in their World), Bouchardeau discusses her ideas about
women and politics, both criticising the mechanisms of party processes and justifying her own position as feminist and national secretary
of a political party. Bouchardeau's critique agrees with other feminist
critiques of politics: political performance and discourse is incompatible both with women's lives, and with the way that feminists
approach politics. There is no place in electoral politics for public
self-criticism and questioning, for the MLF's internal contradictions
and for plurality of strategy.

Bouchardeau examines the formal rituals of politics, and accuses
the structure and format of meetings of preventing any real dialogue
and exchange, and of becoming a sequence of monologues. She also
contends that, in spite of the PSU's declared intentions of collective
decision-making at all levels, at national level, this just doesn't
happen. She attacks the rhetoric of persuasion so essential to the
political speech and text: the speaker at a meeting must dominate
through his or her rhetorical strategies, must speak in an incisive,

logical and confident manner thereby proving his or her superiority. Bouchardeau agrees with MLF arguments that women are frequently intimidated at mixed meetings, frequently lacking the rhetorical training and expertise that vocal men will have had, and that women will go unheard whether or not they have actually spoken, on many occasions. The very procedures of political parties, involving attempts to dominate, convince and persuade, are contrary to feminist practices, and in this, all parties are the same, whether marginal or mainstream or actually in government.

Nevertheless, Bouchardeau believes that it is essential for feminists to keep an active presence inside different parties. She says (*Tribune socialiste*, 14 December 1978):

> political parties exist and we won't be able to change that fact for some time to come. Whether we like it or not, parties are still the place for political intervention where problems of power and the state and local bodies are concerned. If we want these instruments of power to help women instead of burying them, we have to be there, present.

Bouchardeau did not choose one of the big four parties for her presence, however. Her party is not at the centre of the French political stage, but is one which is neither power-holding nor likely to become so. It is a question of compromise: if feminists want to be involved in party politics, they have to weigh up a number of priorities and factors, and choose their party accordingly. For Bouchardeau, the PSU seemed the appropriate compromise precisely because the gaining of power is not a direct issue and the pressures of electoral politics do not weigh as heavily on it as on the PCF and the PS. The PSU, unlike the four major parties, does acknowledge that women need to organise autonomously as well as within the male-dominated political arena; the PSU has premises that are in basic agreement with feminism and MLF analyses, taking account of male/female relations as a social conflict, multiplicity of approach and voice, collective decision-making, desire to experiment, determination to do things differently. In spite of the male resistance to feminism from which the PSU is not exempt, Bouchardeau believes that the PSU's theoretical perspectives mean that the party will be more open to new ideas, more able to listen and to adapt than other parties.

Feminist participation in the PSU seems to be a doubly marginal choice: marginal as feminist and marginal in a small party. However the importance of marginal groups should not be underestimated. The major parties need the support of the minor parties and the more evenly spread the vote, the more important the minor parties are. If these small but significant parties are permeated with feminist ideas and practices, feminism can have a circuitous influence on policies, acting more as a pressure group than as an integral part of the political structure itself, which may feel like less of a betrayal than full involvement in the political system. A compromise of this nature may be more acceptable than membership of the PS or the PCF, easier for the women involved on a day-to-day basis (less hostility) and less like an abandonment of feminist political ideals in the name of cynical expediency.

It is still a compromise however, and a satisfactory feminist political space still escapes women. It is apparently not inside party politics and power structures as they exist today and which show no signs of changing. Classic party political life requires unity, organisation, coherence, all of which feminism resists. Basic incompatibility is reinforced by the way the party resists feminist ideas when they are expressed in any way other than the way chosen by the party. Where power is within reach, the party cannot and will not integrate and accept difference and criticism from within its own ranks. The feminism of the PSU is only possible because of its marginality.

Proximity to power changes parties. When a party is in opposition, it can claim to be feminist with some degree of sincerity: collective work, divergent approaches and many different types of action and intervention can survive when they operate as critical pressure. Once in government, this situation is no longer tenable. Government proposals must convince, not criticise; the programme must be coherent, not many-sided; its front must be united, not dispersed. Once in government, the imperatives of the political world remove politics from the way feminists understand it and from the way they act politically: the attempt to marry new understandings about politics and about women's reality cannot be carried through in a party which governs.[9] The two poles of feminist intervention on the traditional political scene would therefore seem to be co-option by political parties or simply powerlessness, invisibility. Participation in the PSU, important enough to exercise a modicum of influence on parties like the PS, for whom the gaining of power is the central issue, yet far away enough from the powerhouse of politics to maintain a certain integrity may well be an appropriate compromise. Bouchardeau certainly makes a convincing case for it.[10] Yet if this type of intervention, indirect to say the least, is the only type possible for feminists within the existent political structure, it will take decades for feminism to exert any significant influence on the major political groups. There is also the fact that all political life is interdependent and feminism and the minor parties are dependent on the overall political climate in France which is still dominated by elections. Should the Gaullists be returned to power in parliament in 1986 and in the presidency in 1988, then such influence as there is, will, in all probability, evaporate.

The established practices of party politics are disappointingly unreceptive to change, in conflict with feminist practices, and resistant to feminist ideas. Yet many feminists agree with Bouchardeau and believe that the kind of pressure that can be exerted from inside must continue. However, I think it is true to say that the traditional political arena, be it mainstream parties or 'revolutionary' extra-parliamentary groups, takes second place to the search for viable alternative modes of intervention in the autonomous women-only MLF. This search for a different politics has led feminists to confront the problem of organisation and structure, which has been present since the beginning of the MLF and has never been solved (cannot be solved?).

The MLF has always insisted that it is a 'movement' and not an 'organisation'. The distinction may not be clear to some, but it was to feminists in the early 1970s: 'movement' implied dynamism, adaptation, lack of rigidity, while 'organisation' implied hierarchy, immobility, fixed structures. 'Movement' always seemed to fit the shape of the MLF better, with the theoretical perspective of multiplicity mirrored on a practical level by its plurality of approach, the proliferation of groups and the contradictory nature of its various actions. Each group decides on its particular attitude to political institutions and to its own form, can decide on the type of intervention it feels is appropriate, for different degrees of formality are needed for different projects. Feminists who have rejected outright any attempt to change political structures from within have also frequently rejected the calls repeatedly made by others, for the MLF to adopt an organised form. These suggestions have been refused on the grounds that any kind of formal organisation would deform the nature of the

MLF, bringing in notions of leadership, the need for a coherent platform which would deny the movement's diversity and egalitarianism. Yet while it is fear of this kind of deformation that makes feminists refuse to organise as a formal, integrated body, it is also paradoxically this very refusal that leaves their theoretical and practical achievements open to co-option: lack of formal organisation makes it possible for others to step in and claim feminist actions and ideas as their own.

It has been suggested[11] that the MLF plays a deliberate kind of co-option game, in which feminists have the ideas and then these ideas are turned into reforms by political parties. The MLF keeps its integrity intact and doesn't spoil its idealism with pragmatism, while at the same time changes are made in favour of women. French feminists have been more adamant than British feminists over the rejection of reforms, have never formalised certain demands as the British women's movement has,[12] and have not really distinguished between reform and co-option. French feminists do not trust political parties and hold that the patriarchal structures of political parties will always destroy the revolutionary meaning of feminism, and that feminist demands, once taken up by others, will only serve the interests of those others, be it the Communist Party or the state. Removing demands from the overall context of the MLF distorts the meaning of those demands while giving the superficial impression of taking feminist positions into account. Even so, the refusal to adopt any kind of formal organised shape means that the MLF cannot effectively defend the demands that feminists make, cannot re-place, for instance, the abortion issue in a 'feminist global context' because there is fundamentally no agreement about what that context actually is.

This question of organisation has been the most difficult and frustrating of questions to confront. Invisible and powerless or distorted and co-opted: is there no third option? From quite early on, some women were concerned with over-emphasising rejection of organisation without considering that there might be some positive aspects to think about. The 'ghetto', silent and powerless, was a recurrent image. As mentioned above, *Psych et Po* (*des femmes en mouvements mensuelle*, No. 8–9, 1978) refused this image as male-inspired and male-created:

It is precisely Parties and Power who say that the women's

> movement is marginal, that is, in their margins . . . as soon as
> there is an attempt to refuse, a gesture of rupture, of
> transformation, there is a word stuck to it by those in power:
> marginal, to limit and close in what is happening . . . We're not in
> the margins, we are working to explode the system that says we
> are marginal.

For *Psych et Po*, it is a question of re-centring energy and perspective, and recognition by authority (the Father) is not at stake. *Psych et Po* rejected any sort of participation in political parties, saying that it is impossible to fight against something while being part of it. They further suggest that by entering the masculine world of politics, and by accepting to act and speak from within pre-established boundaries, these women function in the framework of masculine values. The most successful women politicians have been those who have adopted the rules and behaviour of their male colleagues and have not questioned the nature of politics: Simone Veil, Giscard's Minister of Health, was even called the strong man of his government. *Psych et Po* feel that once women have made the initial compromise of working in a male world, they will never be able to bring a different, specifically feminine perspective to their politics. From this point of view, the number of women in politically powerful positions is irrelevant and Bouchardeau's belief that women must fight for women within the structures that count in patriarchal society, is worthless.

It is clear to see why the MLF refuses to adopt one kind of structure. It is not only for solid theoretical reasons, but also because of the wide variety of response to the question of organisation and the contradictions between some of the responses. Plurality of approach is positive as well as negative: while effective concerted action is difficult, dispersed, simultaneous action is easy, and feminists can exercise influence at different levels and on different terrains of social life. By refusing to channel feminist struggles into one political form, all options are left open, and women can engage in activity in whichever way they find appropriate, whether it would fit into a 'classic' definition of what is political or not. In this sense then, feminism can be seen as a structural chameleon, which is definitely a strength rather than a weakness.

This strength lies in the fact that all degrees of visibility and invisibility can be there at the same time. Sometimes invisibility from power can be positive and safe: those who would attack feminism can't look at all sides at once, don't know where to look and can't recognise what they see.

The limited or diluted influence that feminism can have on the political structures in place is a direct consequence of the multiplicity of the MLF's analysis and formation. To develop a viable strategy, a political movement must have clear goals and must work out a strategy in term of the political system in which it operates. Feminism is too dispersed and fragmented a movement, too diverse in its approaches, too vague about the kind of society that feminists envisage, to be able to function effectively in the political world of France as it is today. This is compounded by the hostility of those involved in established political practices to the attempts made by feminists to act upon these practices from within. By trying to change the rules of the political game, they have been excluded from playing, for those who make the rules are those who decide on the players.

Yet again, it is paradoxically the multiplicity of feminism that makes it significant politically. Practices are adapted from unions (strikes, marches, demonstrations), from university life (seminars, study groups, workshops), from revolutionary politics, from social work. These have fused into an eclectic style of political activity which mirrors the eclectic composition of the movement. The variety of actions carried out, the different pressures applied, combine to form a visible and significant movement, bringing feminism onto the political stage and forcing political parties to account for women in the elaboration of their programmes. The problem facing feminists does not change: how to reconcile women's lives, feminist practice and party politics. This is persistently sought and equally persistently elusive. The hope lies in the combination of autonomous structures plus feminists acting against all odds inside male-dominated structures. This combination, feminists hope, will, slowly but irrevocably, force men to see that feminism is a serious political commitment and not a footnote to party programmes, at the same time as the women's movement builds its own political style and develops its own analyses.

The issue of organisation makes women think about what feminism actually *is*: unlike a party, it isn't something you can join or be kicked out of, resign from. No one has the prerogative of saying that *you* are feminist and *you* are not. It cannot exclude women who call themselves feminists. If feminism is at base a practice of solidarity with all women, then all practices that favour women are useful, and disagreement among feminists may not matter at all. This may seem an expedient attitude to have, based on believing that differences will never be overcome, but I think that it is more than that. Unity is not the goal, never has been and no doubt never will be. The image that remains in my mind that illustrates the MLF's thinking about structure is one suggested by Florence Kennedy in the film *Born in Flames:* if you were to be attacked, would you rather be attacked by one, unified lion or by five thousand mice?

CHAPTER 7

Feminism in Socialist France[1]

In May 1981, the socialists came to power in France after an absence of 25 years from office, and for the first time since the foundation of the Fifth Republic. Feminists actively supported the non-Communist Left during the election campaign, with even *Psych et Po*, in a reversal of their former position, calling for women to vote Mitterrand from the first ballot to ensure the presence of the Left in the second ballot.

The excitement at François Mitterrand's election to the presidency and the overwhelming majority won by the PS in the new French parliament marked May 1981 as a pivotal point for many sections of the French population, who now saw the chance for radical change. For feminists too, the change of government was heralded as a breath of fresh air: they hoped that the socialist government would work both to improve women's situation in society and also to provide a more positive space for the MLF to occupy. Feminists hoped that the socialists would listen with a more attentive ear to what they had to say and to the demands that they were making.

May 1981, then, seemed to provide a good point for feminists to pause for reflection, to think about what the women's movement had become over its first decade and to think about its potential for the future. This final chapter will look at the changing situation for feminism in France since the socialists have been in power, with particular attention to the relationship of feminism to power and to the questions that have been raised since 1981 when this relationship was altered quite significantly.

Psych et Po calls for a woman to vote

No doubt the most obviously important action taken by the socialist government in favour of women has been the establishment of a new Ministry for Women's Rights (*le Ministère des Droits de la Femme*).[2] Under the previous government, President Valéry Giscard d'Estaing had set up a 'Secretariat concerned with women's condition' (*le Secrétariat à la Condition Féminine*) and appointed a well known journalist, Françoise Giroud, to head it. The goal of the Secretariat was, somewhat vaguely, to make recommendations to the Prime Minister's office about changes and improvements that could be made for women in France. Madame Giroud, after an initial hesitation about serving in a government which she did not support, accepted the appointment and after two years produced a detailed programme of priorities for actions that could be taken to benefit women, called *Projet Pour les Femmes* (Project for Women), in which she set out 101 proposals in favour of changes in 'women's condition'. The Secretary had no budget of her own for initiating any reforms or campaigns and her proposals were intended only as recommendations to the Prime Minister, who could then act on them or not. When her programme was produced, it attracted a lot of attention in the press: *Le Monde* (17 May 1976) devoted a page to it, other newspapers made a variety of positive or sarcastic comments about it, all the political parties pronounced on it, and feminists were sceptical. Denise Cacheux, a Socialist Member of Parliament said (*Le Monde* 5 June 1976) 'the secretary concerned with women's condition is nothing but an alibi for a right-wing government which has made up its mind not to question the economic mechanisms nor the structures that demand profound changes'; while Martine Storti wrote in *Libération* (28 May 1976) that 'these "feminist" concessions do not mask the underlying philosophy of the project: that is, the integration of women into men's world, men's models, and the sharing of a kind of power and a kind of values that women have shown that they don't want.' Madame Giroud's proposals were accepted and approved by parliament in principle, but no action was ever taken to realise any of her suggestions and her post disappeared in a cabinet reshuffle a few months later. She was replaced by a 'Delegate' representing women, Nicole Pasquier, whose ignorance of, and insensitivity to, women's problems was embarrassingly revealed at her first press conference. The reporter from *Libération* (15 November 1976) was scathing:

We can credit her with sympathy, with a smile and with the best intentions. But she doesn't know either what to say, or what she can or wants to do. To our questions, she mostly replied by saying: 'I'm not fully in the picture about this, but I will look into it', or 'You're right, its an important issue' or 'I will try to do something about it, believe me' . . .

Nicole Pasquier was subsequently replaced by Monique Pelletier as Spokeswoman for Women and the Family attached to the Prime Minister's office, whose role was so clearly nothing more than a token, that nobody paid her any attention.

The socialist creation of a Ministry for Women's Rights was clearly of a different order. Its initial budget was very small (94.28 million francs, or 0.025 per cent of the total budget) but there were still enough funds to give out, projects to initiate and legislation to be fought for.

The woman chosen as Minister was Yvette Roudy, a long-standing socialist activist but not sympathetic to MLF-style feminism. Nevertheless, her analysis of women's oppression went further than any government has admitted before. Roudy declared that the goal of her Ministry was to intervene wherever necessary to correct discrimination of all kinds against women. In her definition of discrimination, she was ready to take account of attitudes towards, and perceptions of, women, and acknowledged that these attitudes and the structures that operate to keep women subordinate to men are deeply-rooted in French life. She therefore accepted the need to work on informing and 'sensitising' the public to specifically women's issues as well as fighting for changes at an institutional level.

The Ministry's work is organised around three areas: information, professional and skilled training, and legislation. One of the first campaigns started by the Ministry was to give information about contraception to young people. The campaign included television 'spots' about responsible sexual behaviour, shot by feminist film-maker Agnès Varda. The Ministry also fought for, and eventually obtained, provision for abortion to be reimbursed by Social Security (the equivalent of abortion on the National Health in Britain), although the limitations of the abortion law still exist; they proposed a controversial anti-sexist law in 1983, modelled on the 1972 anti-racist law, aiming to give women legal recourse against offensive public images of women;[3] they published a booklet as a Guide to Women's Rights and distributed this free; they subsidise various independent feminist projects and have supported many independent feminist initiatives, much like the Greater London Council in London; and they set up their own projects, such as the revision of images of women in school books and the examination of the image of women in advertising. Most recently in 1983–4, they have been working on a law concerning 'professional equality' (equality at work), and have encouraged the setting up of Feminist Studies in higher education, together with the Ministry of National Education and the Ministry of Research and Industry.

All in all, it is a reform-based enterprise in the best tradition. The Ministry encourages sensitivity to women's issues in the workplace, has set up information centres throughout France and encourages women to enter professions traditionally defined as male preserves, to seek qualifications in the sciences, technology and medicine, and to train as engineers, mechanics and computer programmers – to give women and girls equal opportunities. The Minister claims that she is working towards the disappearance of her own Ministry – for if sexism, inequality and discrimination disappeared from people's minds and from concrete everyday situations and structures, there would be no need for a Ministry for Women's Rights.

This very positive appraisal of the Ministry must, however, be tempered with the problems that its appearance has raised. Feminists inside the PS have found themselves increasingly marginalised in the party to the point that many of the *courant G* have now left the party, while the Ministry becomes the official voice of socialist feminism. The feminist current had wanted to develop a feminist analysis that could take its place as a global political analysis on the same footing as the other socialist currents, and bring the question of women's oppression to the attention of the PS as a whole. Accused of trying to create a feminist 'ghetto', they were in fact attempting to avoid this problem, by showing that feminists do not want to comment exclusively on contraception or housework, but want to bring a feminist perspective to every aspect of social life. The establishment of a Ministry for Women's Rights has meant the kind of ghettoisation that Roudy had used as an argument against the *courant G:* certain issues become defined as 'women's' issues and are pushed towards the Ministry rather than dealt with by the party as a whole. The PS can thus successfully avoid taking on the real challenge of feminism, and

129

the Ministry is criticised by some women as being only a skin-deep gesture of appeasement to feminism rather than a real attempt to change male/female relations.[4]

Roudy's style of leadership has also been heavily criticised by women both inside and outside the PS. She was not one of the women in the party most committed to women, and had been an active critic of feminism for the familiar reason that feminism divides and disperses the struggle against capitalism. Yet since becoming Minister, she is taking centre stage as a feminist and is taking personal credit for actions and ideas that would have been unthinkable without the struggle of the MLF. The Ministry publishes a monthly newsletter/ magazine called *Citoyennes à part entière* (Fully-fledged citizens) in which Roudy figures as a major star, with pictures of her liberally scattered through the magazine and her words and speeches quoted and reprinted respectfully. A star system has been created of professional feminists[5] with the Ministry at its heart and with the MLF wondering what happened and what to make of it.

The PS victory has had a further effect on feminism within the party. Until 1981, the PS, as has been said, was organised in the form of diverse currents, each defining itself as socialist but each bringing different perspectives to the party. While in opposition, the PS was keen to attract a wide variety of people, wanted to be a catch-all party and contrast its openness and tolerance with the doctrinaire Communist Party. But once in government, this changed. Prior to the annual PS Congress at Valence in October 1981, the three major currents (Mitterrand, Mauroy and the CERES) came to an agreement, deciding to put forward a common proposal rather than maintaining their differences in separate proposals, as had previously been the case. Michel Rocard's current was also obliged to support the proposal if he didn't want to lose all power and be pushed to the margins of the party, or be pushed out. The Congress at Valence was proclaimed a massive victory for party unity. The voice of dissent – the feminist voice – went unreported, unnoticed, as indeed their own proposal went unvoted. In their journal, they noted how the PS could tolerate a feminist presence while in opposition, but that everything was now different. The majority of women who had been involved in the former feminist current left the party. Attempts by those who stayed to keep up their critical pressure in diverse ways have been blocked and frustrated; only their tenacity and their long-term commitment to feminism keep them there.

Now in power, the PS no longer needs the catch-all appeal of the different currents. Far from constituting the basis for a future, pluralist, socialist society, the currents are more of a hindrance to party unity, which becomes the main requirement of a party in government. A party in opposition and a party in government have different needs and that which had previously been acceptable and accepted as theoretical diversity and richness becomes a handicap. The PS has systematically blocked any potential openings for a feminist critique in the context of general party debate. The attempt to form a feminist current in the party, which should theoretically be possible, was tolerated at first but became embarrassing and cumbersome once the party took office; and clearly, the more entrenched the PS becomes in established power structures, the wider the gulf between the party and the women's movement will grow.

The PS in power is showing, on the one hand, at least a gesture of understanding towards the need for women to participate fully in political life (for instance, the PS accepts a quota of at least 20 per cent women candidates on lists of party political candidates), but has been criticised for making outrageously partisan appointments for women, on the other. Those informal yet influential posts – personal staff in political cabinets, advisers and parliamentary attachés – are filled with the wives and daughters of socialist politicians in the most blatant way. *Libération* (8 March 1984) delighted in flitting through the *Gazette du Parlement* (Parliamentary Gazette) to see not only the relative proportion of women to men (1:3), their relative roles (women tend to be secretaries or public relations officers), but also who the women actually were. Access to power is totally controlled by party hierarchy, those women who had previously not had access to significant political posts are still excluded, and feminists are not finding promotion within the party any more than they did before.

A further point worth making is of the contradiction of having on the one hand a Ministry for Women's Rights and on the other a government body (headed initially by Georgina Dufoix) designed to promote and defend the family:[6] the way that these two bodies affect each other and contradict each other's aims will reflect on the PS's credibility where women are concerned.

For the MLF, the change of government in 1981 opened up new questions. While the internal dynamic of the movement – *Psych et Po*, political lesbianism, splits between groups and individuals as well as the positive side of new projects and the strengthening of existent initiatives – continued with periods of greater and lesser activity, the relation of the women's movement to the French political world around it altered significantly. The MLF began to reassess its relation to political institutions and, through this reassessment, began to rethink features of the MLF that had been part of the movement for so long that they were taken for granted. For instance, the question of organisation and structure became central to MLF thinking in this way.

While the Right had been in power, it had been relatively easy for the MLF as a movement to decide on its attitude to power and to organisation: when those who hold power are defined as the enemy, a stance of opposition is the straightforward position to adopt. Because the enemy were in power, suspicion of reform and feminist hostility to government was the norm and any approval of government reform (such as the abortion law reform) was tempered with criticisms of the law's inevitable limitations and doubts about its sincerity.

Now that those who might be considered friends are in power, the MLF has been impelled to think again about its attitude to reform and to its own form of organisation. The paradox of the structural fluidity of the MLF, under scrutiny once more, is that while it appears to hold back the development of feminist strategy, it also allows it to adapt and reconsider concepts, structures and attitudes as feminist experience changes and as the political conditions evolve. Feminist thinking about the relationship of the women's movement to the socialist government began almost immediately. Signs of this new reflection were quickly found in the feminist press, from approaches to theorising about women and the state (in *Nouvelles Questions feministes*), to debate about the internal structuring of the women's movement (*La Revue d'en face* Nos 11 and 12 and others). Certain women have argued for positive links with the government, considering that honest, public support of the socialist government by feminists is essential. Françoise Ducrocq, for instance, calls for a clear position vis-à-vis the government and vis-à-vis the structure of the women's movement, seeing the need to set up feminist structures which would be as autonomous as possible yet have strong links to public institutions (such as universities, various Ministries, etc.). Marie-Jo Dhavernas and Françoise Picq also argued for a greater degree of structuration at a national level, not replacing the small group but adding to it. Marie-Jo Dhavernas asked (*La Revue d'en face* No. 11, p.35) whether in fact the kind of thinking she felt was needed would only be possible by a 'new political generation, or by women who have fewer memories than we do . . .'. Françoise Picq (*La Revue d'en face* No. 11, p. 24) felt that 'we need to set up structures where collective decisions can be taken, without power play or manipulation and respecting minority positions. Why shouldn't women be capable of this?'

This desire to engage in a new self-criticism and examination was prompted by developments both internal and external to the MLF: after the acquisition of the MLF's name by *Psych et Po*, the rest of the women's movement began, in meetings and in print, to pose again the question of structure and ask whether the structurelessness of the first ten years was going to be appropriate as a form for the MLF in its second decade. There was a growing feeling that the MLF needed something to change so that it could adapt effectively to the new situation. The excitement of discovery and the enormous mobilising power of the abortion campaign had carried the movement through its first few years, but this kind of vigour and momentum inevitably exhausts itself and must be replaced with something of a more durable nature.

Women still prefer to function through small, informal group structures for reasons that don't change: rejection of hierarchy and leadership, desire for each woman to be able to develop her own potential without risk of ridicule or neglect. The small group structure has been extremely positive for individual women and for the MLF as a whole, providing a context of support and allowing a kind of discussion that would be impossible in large meetings. The different interests of different groups have permitted development of simultaneous projects in varying fields of activity – inside trade unions, political parties, and at the workplace; in the building of alternative structures and networks of women; and in different local projects.

It must be remembered, though, that these groups were not only formed for positive reasons but for the practical reason that large groups of feminists often find it impossible to work together.[7] Diversity often equals fragmentation caused by disagreement: the mutual support within the small groups is not often repeated in larger formations. And although there is no call for a united MLF, any attempt to work in collective ways that co-ordinate different groups is made very difficult. Disagreement ends in a split between women, taking on the shape of personal hostility. The MLF is riddled with such personal/political hostilities between individual women as well as between groups. The effect can seem ridiculous, petty or comical from the outside, but is a sad comment on sisterhood. The situation is such that, although in the early and mid-1970s the diverse groups were able to come together for certain actions and campaigns, or for specific events, this has not been possible for at least five years now.

Structurelessness places great strain on feminists as far as identity and identification are concerned. One positive aspect of having 'a clear political line' and party structure is that it gives members a point of reference: they can say 'I am a member of the PCF or the Ecology Party or whatever – because I believe the following'. Feminists have to go further than this. It is not enough to say that you are a feminist because you believe that women are oppressed, but you have to say what kind of feminist you are: identity must be created and re-created not only in relation to other forms of politics but in relation to other feminisms.[8] By identification, I mean that the non-feminist public cannot tell what or who constitutes the MLF, or what this or that feminist comment means in different contexts, when spoken by different women and so on. If a woman claims to be speaking for the MLF, this will not be doubted by most people, only by those who are aware of the ins and outs of the MLF's complicated life. Among feminists, it has always been tacitly understood and sometimes explicitly agreed that any statement of any kind was to be made in the name of the speaker or in the name of a particular group, adding 'as part of the women's liberation movement' to their name. Nobody can claim to speak for the whole movement. *Psych et Po*, the only group to understand from early on the need for public identification, did just this, and solved the problem for themselves in their own way. They seemed for a short time to have made themselves the spokes-women for the MLF. This was only possible because of the lack of structuring of the MLF, because of the movement's insistence on diversity and its refusal to adopt any kind of representative forma-tion. These same reasons make the MLF susceptible to co-option by political parties although in a different way from that of *Psych et Po*. However political parties also try to turn feminism into what they want it to mean, to suit their own needs. Every political party needs to have some perspective on feminism – although it may be one of ridicule. Each political party will claim to represent the interests of women better than any other, and tend to see this in the context of the family or of the working class: the PCF calls itself the party of women's liberation; the centre Right, under Giscard, prided itself on its powerless Secretariat; Jacques Chirac and the Gaullist Right claim to work for women in the family; the socialists can attempt to become synonymous with feminism through the Ministry for Women's Rights; and there is no-one who can contradict these claims on behalf of the MLF in a way that will carry weight with political parties, with the media and the press, and with the general public.

It was with these questions in mind that I went to talk to women in the women's movement in Paris in October 1984. Restricted by time, by the availability of people to talk to (for instance Yvette Roudy and her advisers were in China) and further restricted by catching the flu on my second day there, I still managed to discuss a number of these issues with a variety of women, that show some – although by no means all – of the current thinking in the women's movement and show the alteration of focus, of attitudes and of structure that has taken place over the last three years.

The discussions I had with different women reflected the feeling that I already had, that the entire atmosphere has changed in France over the past two or three years, and that the new relation to power has been instrumental in bringing about these changes. As a result of what women said to me, some of my ideas about the French women's movement were altered, and others were confirmed. Mostly what was confirmed for me was the fact that there are as many feminisms as there are feminists; that divergence of opinion and priority can be both a source of richness and a source of paralysis; and that divisions between feminists, however important they may seem from within and however painful they may be to experience, may not, in a wider perspective, matter at all: as long as women are working and thinking in small groups and as individuals, it may not matter at all that the huge sweep of the movement has disappeared.

I came away feeling neither pessimistic nor optimistic about 'the future of feminism' in France or elsewhere, but more convinced than ever that even thinking in these terms is not useful. Feminism must be seen in a long-term perspective – a lifetime's commitment on an individual scale, and as part of centuries of struggle on a collective scale. I was also confirmed in my belief that it is impossible to consider feminism divorced from its political and cultural context; it does not develop in isolation from the specific political and social world around it, but rather as an integral part of this specific setting –

the specificity of French feminist theory comes from the specificity of French culture, notably from the place of Marxism and psychoanalysis within that culture. The way that feminism in France will develop is tied in the same way to the way that political and social life in France will evolve. France in 1984 has been experiencing the crisis of the Socialist Government, increased unemployment, the decline of the Communist Party, and the alarming rise of the French National Front (FN) led by Jean-Marie Le Pen. The space that feminists can carve out for feminism depends, for instance, on who will be returned to the National Assembly after the legislative elections in 1986, and to the presidency in 1988. Should the Gaullists be returned to power as is widely predicted (but which is not as inevitable as we may fear) women may lose the rights that it has taken so long to win – Chirac has already spoken out against the reimbursement of abortion by social security, and the next step would be to repeal the 1975 abortion law altogether. But this is speculation.

The discussions took various forms and covered similar but not identical ground. As it would be impossible to reproduce the 10½ hours of taped conversation, I have thought it best to proceed by theme, with a mixture of direct quotation and synthesis of the substance of what was said over the three days.

'You don't make a movement with money alone'

I obviously wanted to ask women about the continuing fortunes of *Psych et Po*, seeing that this subject had generated so much attention for so long. Nobody seemed particularly interested in taking up the story, or even knew whether there was a story to take up. Nobody seemed able to tell me whether or not *Psych et Po* as a political group even existed any more and nobody seemed to care.

Nadja Ringart: I really don't want to know about them or talk about them. They only matter when they do something that concerns us like reprinting *Le Torchon brûle*, which was the last thing they did – that was dreadful, a real dispossession.
Obviously they still exist as a bookshop and as a publishing company . . .
Liliane Kandel: As long as they do what they do in their own name, that's OK. They used to sign MLF – 'Women from the

MLF publish' or 'the MLF publishes' but now there's been a change to a more impresario-like 'Antoinette Fouque presents' . . .

Françoise Ducrocq: The last time they were really in evidence was during the May '81 elections, and then when they tried to turn International Women's Day into a paid holiday for women – well it didn't work – they spent a fortune on the campaign.

Nadja Ringart: It shows that you can't form a movement with money alone. Let's not talk about it any more.

Clearly then, there are scars, felt most acutely by women whose texts had been reprinted by the *éditions des femmes*, women who were directly implicated in the battle against them. But also clearly, *Psych et Po* is not a major concern today, does not command the same response as it used to. Certain things have changed within the group: Antoinette has moved to California; Hélène Cixous has distanced herself from the group; the *hebdo* has ceased publication; and recruitment to the publishing company is done through public advertising rather than as political appointments.

*   *   *

The lack of permeability between *des femmes* and feminism is absolute. The second irrevocable split is between radical feminists and the women who now organise separately as radical lesbians as described in Chapter 1. The lesbian movement, still in its early stages, defines itself independently of both the mixed homosexual movement – the FHAR – and the MLF. What the women involved hope to see is the creation of a sense of community among lesbians, and they expressed the desire to analyse all problems (for instance racism) from a lesbian perspective. One important step has been the establishment of the lesbian archives in Paris, a documentation centre containing books, articles, magazines about lesbianism and by lesbians from many different countries. As well as being a documentation centre, the hope is that it will also operate as a place where women can discuss things, exchange ideas and, generally meet.

*   *   *

It is clear, then, that by 1984 the MLF was no longer what it had been.

Many women suggested that the changed movement could be seen in terms of a coming to adulthood after a prolonged adolescence, so that certain joyful aspects (and many painful ones) had gone, but that this aging is necessary and was long overdue.

Unthinkable without socialism?

CD: How do you think that the women's movement has changed since 1981?

Françoise Ducrocq: I think that it's true to say that what we're most involved in doing at the moment is centred on research and study – I'm not sure that we have any concrete results to speak of yet.

Nadja Ringart: To a certain extent we have. Groups have become structured in a certain way, so that we could get subsidies –

Liliane Kandel: and that would have been unthinkable without socialism . . .

Nadja Ringart: Well, how do we know? We never asked for money before, apart from a couple of groups, whom we called 'reformist' with great disdain.

Françoise Ducrocq: No, but the new government did make a difference: it has been a breath of fresh air for feminists. We now have a way of being heard, there is a link, an attention that wasn't there before 1981. When you've got women like Huguette Bouchardeau and Simone Iff[9] in positions of power, things change. And we've changed too, on our side there's been the introduction of a reality principle in our politics that we didn't have before – the end of our Utopian discourse.

Liliane Kandel: I think it was Marie-Jo Dhavernas who said that socialism is all very well, it's good for us, but it has made us age by 20 years in 3 months.

Françoise Ducrocq: No bad thing either.

*   *   *

Danielle Haase-Dubosc: I think that having friends in power has changed many things. The women's movement was always an opposition movement, a doubly opposition movement, rejecting all structure and so on – and then all of a sudden this changed. We suddenly had a government in which there was supposedly a place for women. It has forced many of us into silence because there is no way in which we can oppose this government – we *do* think that it's doing something for women, and it supposedly supports the platform we all fought for. We still have criticisms to make, but to voice them would be to be guilty of lack of loyalty. I also think that we had become so used to our anarchic way of functioning that to break the bonds there, in order to constitute other forms for action has been a serious psychological and political shock and a problem for many women. But this is precisely what has been happening.

*   *   *

The *courant G* were the most cynical in their opinion of the government. While they acknowledged that the Ministry for Women's Rights did useful work in certain areas, such as women's work, vocational training and information, they were generally negative about the government. 'Whenever I see Mitterrand I come out in spots,' said one woman. Another woman explained: 'The men who are now in power were our comrades, our friends. We've discussed everything with them for years – and then the PS gets into power and they don't want to know, they don't want to share their power with women, especially with women who don't toe their line.'

The women from the Ministry

CD: Do you think that the Ministry is taking over, or replacing the women's movement?
Marie-Jo Dhavernas: No, I don't think so. The women in the Ministry aren't women who are or were involved in the MLF on the whole. They are women from the PS – and not feminists from the PS.
Françoise Gollain: I think that in some places, for instance the West of France where I'm from, the Ministry tends to replace the women's movement. It provides the only focus for a lot of women there who don't know or hear about the groups and

places that you've been talking about, but who do know about the Ministry.

Françoise Duroux: The problem with the Ministry is that they operate in a vacuum – they don't really know what's going on in the movement; they consult a few women, women they know, in an ad hoc fashion and think that that's enough. This ends up replacing the dialogue that there really ought to be between the Ministry and the women's movement.

Oristelle Bonis: There's also the question of money, funding from the Ministry. I think that the major split between feminists is not between intellectuals and activists but between those who have successfully negotiated money and those who haven't.

*   *   *

Rosi Braidotti: Obviously the Ministry is leaving its mark, its imprint on the women's movement. What we've done is establish a femocracy without thinking about what we're doing . . .

Silence and success

Françoise Ducrocq: People say that we don't need feminism any more, we've won.

Nadja Ringart: This idea is used to shut us up. But what have we really won? What have we got that they can't take away?

Liliane Kandel: Some of us are studying the social effects of feminism and there clearly *are* some ideas that have found their place in society thanks to the MLF and are now irreversible. There are ideas now held by women who would never dream of calling themselves feminists, a sort of *féminisme ordinaire* (everyday feminism) . . .

Françoise Ducrocq: Yes, but look at what happens when you talk to younger women – when I talk to my students about women's oppression, they don't see it like that – they say, well we've got contraception, we've got abortion, or they say, my bloke isn't like that, or I've never been discriminated against because I'm a woman . . .

*   *   *

Rosi Braidotti: It would be terrible if feminism just became another dogma to pass on to our daughters.

*   *   *

The conversations ranged over a number of issues: young women and the 'renewal' of the MLF (Nadja Ringart: 'a catastrophe'; Danielle Haase-Dubosc: 'younger women are there, not many of them, but they are there . . .'; Rosi Braidotti: 'we're not renewing ourselves, its always the same women . . .'); about what is happening outside Paris – which nobody seemed to know and which was symptomatic of the lack of contact between feminist groups that everyone mentioned; about style (Colette Guillaumin: 'Everyone has to be *branché*, plugged in, hip, cool as though these things have an independent existence, as though there's real choice . . .'); about anti-semitism. There was an understandable reluctance to talk about difficulties between women either individually or between groups and a reluctance to raise issues that had originally caused a split and that were still potentially explosive (money, political lesbianism). It was as if talking about it in order to inform me might have re-opened the particular quarrel, which nobody wanted to do.

There were several topics that I wanted to raise but which didn't seem to interest anyone particularly, unless I just expressed myself badly: I wanted to ask about issues that are important in the women's movement in Britain and that seemed to me to be absent from the French women's movement – the peace movement and Greenham; racism within the women's movement. When I mentioned racism, it was either addressed in terms of immigrant women or in terms of supporting groups fighting female sexual mutilation – which again shows a different cultural context from the terms of the British debate on racism, and also shows a lack of awareness (or an acceptance) of the fact that the MLF is overwhelmingly a white women's movement.

This attitude was noticed two years ago at a conference on women's studies held at Toulouse in November 1982, which brought together 750 women. In her report on the conference, Irish feminist Ailbhe Smyth noted that 'both *class* and *race* seemed to have been evacuated by – for once – common and totally tacit consent.' She went on to comment on one session on women and education:

I felt that we were there to discuss how we could improve our own already very privileged situation, and that all those millions of women – in France and elsewhere – who have little or no access to those privileges – were not really the concern of research *by* women except, of course, in so far as they are *objects* of that research. The impact of our intellectual activity on the daily lives of 'ordinary' women was, with certain very honourable exceptions, *not* a suitable subject for discussion. I contracted a fairly severe form of 'ivory-towerism' i.e. a sense of living in the rarer reaches of abstraction, where questions such as 'In what way does what we are doing directly or indirectly influence/ change women's lives?' seemed crude and out of place. Such questions when they *were* asked produced a glazed expression . . .[10]

This kind of elitism was not identified as a problem by the women I spoke to, except indirectly, when women spoke of the lack of contact between groups, or of a split between intellectuals and activists in the movement (although, again, class and race were not overtly mentioned in this context). Some women seemed to feel that the women's movement didn't exist any more in France and had been replaced by women's studies . . .

The women's movement *does* exist in France, but it exists differently: the impact of the change of government not only altered women's relation to political institutions but also the dynamic within the movement. The ambivalence that many women seem to share about the changing shape of the women's movement does not prevent general satisfaction at seeing financial support given to a variety of projects. There are the inevitable personal grievances and resentments about who gets the money and how much, who gets the jobs and for how long – these new animosities are added to the old. Nancy Huston had noted in *Histoires d'elles* in 1978 that 'the paths of feminism constantly split off and divide; you have to make choices and enemies', and this is as true now as it was then. But, from a different perspective, beyond the problems of fragmentation, there is an impressive range of feminist groups and projects in existence, both within and outside institutional settings, both with financial support from the Ministry and without it.

Feminism is dead. Long live feminist studies?

The area of feminist activity that everyone noted as particularly flourishing is research, and women's studies. This focus on research rather than on more 'practical' actions was praised by some and criticised by others. Marie-Jo Dhavernas pointed out that the women labelled as 'intellectuals' were the same women who had marched, demonstrated, signed petitions, been arrested, attended meetings and written articles since the beginning of the 1970s, and she felt that the dichotomy between intellectual work and practical work was artificial. What had changed was the terrain of the struggle: some women felt that writing and research was their chosen area of activism, others felt that it wasn't. The problem with this 'choice' of the terrain for the struggle was the accompanying feeling of exclusivity and that research was taking priority over other forms of action.

While certain women concerned with research had already been active in university-based groups (such as the *groupe d'études féministes*, known as the GEF, in Paris, the Centre Lyonnaise d'Etudes Féministes in Lyon and the Centre d'Etudes Féministes de l'Université de Provence in Aix-en-Provence), the impulse to develop further the scope of feminist research seems to date from 1982. In January 1982 the Ministry of Research and Technology organised a national conference on research, for which the feminist contributions had been in preparation for some months. One result of this conference was the decision to hold the *Femmes, féminisme, recherches* (Women, Feminism, Research) conference at Toulouse in December 1982. At Toulouse, the Parisian regional committee proposed that a national women's studies association should be set up, but this was rejected, and the APEF – *Association pour les Etudes Féministes* – (Feminist Studies Association) was set up as a Paris-based association. Other regional associations have since been created but are at present less active than the APEF. Françoise Duroux explained the goals of the APEF: 'What we aim for is the creation of a situation for feminist studies and research where there is the most co-operation and the least competition possible. We try to provide information about what we're all doing, circulate information, provide details about seminars that are going on in the Paris area and so on.'

A further result of the Toulouse conference was the founding of research groups within the CNRS (the main research institute with government funding) focussing on diverse aspects of feminist research, which seem to be flourishing today.

In spite of the desire for maximum co-operation, even within feminist studies there are apparently problems. Ailbhe Smyth noted at Toulouse: 'an all-pervasive sense of divisiveness: Parisians vs. "provincials"; research institutes vs. universities, and both of these vs. women working in alternative groups and contexts; psychologists vs. sociologists, philosophers vs. psychoanalysts' etc.

A further problem was pointed out concerning the infiltration of feminist ideas in educational institutions. The idea that women in university jobs whose posts are secure would pave the way for other women to come in, has taken a beating. One university woman became very angry when talking about the way in which some of her colleagues responded – or failed to respond – to the challenge presented by the 1981 elections – when the possibility to *do* something was there at last:

What really makes me furious is the sheer duplicity of some women. You know, they complain and complain about how they can't do anything and so on, and yet now that they have the chance to change things, they won't, because of their careers. There has been a real display of cowardice. When the CNRS changed its structure, feminists already working there should have pushed for money, for posts, and so on, – and they just didn't, except for Christine Delphy and one or two others. It's as if there was a split between themselves as feminists and themselves at work. These women are so cynical and so cowardly, it disgusts me . . .

A case where there was great disappointment was over the allocation of four university jobs, to be appointed in different academic disciplines but with the added focus on feminist studies. The way that the appointments were made astonished feminists. For each post (at Paris VII, Rennes, Toulouse and Nantes) an appointments committee was set up. It was announced that in the selection process 'knowledge of, and competence in, feminism will be taken into account'. A comparable statement concerning an appointment in, for instance, history, would have been treated with the ridicule it deserves ('A knowledge of and competence in history will be taken into account' . . .).

Marie-Jo Dhavernas: This incredible lack of rigour in choosing the person for the job shows their contempt for feminism.
Françoise Duroux: We (the APEF) weren't consulted; nobody who might have been able to judge in any way was consulted. No one is really competent to judge ability in feminist studies because there have never been any feminist studies. Some men even applied for the job. In the end each institution made its appointment for internal reasons, which in at least one case was completely unjustified, or at any rate was not the person probably best for the job.
Marie-Jo Dhavernas: So now they can say that there are feminist studies university jobs and there really aren't.

The outcome of the university post appointments was a bitter disappointment and was used by some women to point out the dangers of dependence on those in power. However, an extraordinary range of feminist projects is in existence today with varying degrees of autonomy and varying subsidies from the Ministry for Women's Rights: from significant amounts of money to none at all. Some of these should be mentioned:
– the *Centre de Recherches et d'Information Féministes* (CRIF) – Centre for Feminist Research and Information – was one of the first initiatives to prepare a request for a grant from the Socialist Government in the summer of 1981 and saw its role as a co-ordinating body for feminist studies, and is somewhat in conflict with the APEF.
 – the *Centre audio-visual Simone de Beauvoir* was opened in June 1982. One of the first initiatives to prepare a request for a grant from the Socialist Government (the other was the CRIF), this centre was one of the first new ventures to be established with financial support from the Socialist Government. The centre has several goals: there is an audiovisual documentation service; visual archives; special research is carried out on request; equipment for making videos and films can be rented; films held at the centre are distributed; there are short courses for women on video-making.
 – the *Séminaire Limites-Frontières* (Limits-Frontiers Seminar) has been in existence since 1980, set up by the Association LMF

(*Libération Mouvementée des Femmes* – another way to get round the *Psych et Po* appropriation of MLF). Hélène Rouch explained the goals of the project:

> We wanted women in different disciplines to come together, to see how women in the 'pure' sciences and women in the 'human' sciences could pool their ideas and share knowledge, to understand and to question these bodies of knowledge, see how they are constituted in the first place and how they become closed systems – closures and compartmentalisations that reproduce the hierarchical organisation of our society, which is founded on the exclusion of women.

The feminist press is not flourishing as it was in the late 1970s but is still important as a location for debate and publication of ongoing research. The focus tends not to be so much on the life of the MLF, but on a variety of topics, reflecting the move away from introspection that seems to be the general case of the MLF, and also reflecting the lack of co-ordination between feminist groups (there is little call for a newsletter of the MLF providing general information and contacts). *Nouvelles Questions féministes*, in spite of the problems with its name, the way it was set up and its high price, nevertheless continues to provide a space for the development of feminist theory and publishes a large number of articles by women from other countries. *La Revue d'en face* is one journal whose format was more closely involved with developments inside the MLF and is unlikely to appear again.

> Marie-Jo Dhavernas: There is the question of money, of course, which is paralysing in itself, but also we wanted – and needed – to change the format of the magazine. The *Revue* was always centred on the movement's internal life, its questions and debates, and the movement isn't the same today as it was when we began. There is talk about starting a feminist studies magazine and we – the present collective – couldn't do it. We've been working together for so long, and the collective is based on our personal affinities and interests. A feminist studies journal should have a wider-based collective. We want long, quite fully-developed articles, and we aren't yet sure about what will happen.

The *Cahiers du GRIF*, however, began publication again after a four-year interlude.

Rosi Braidotti: The *Cahiers'* collective is now based in Paris rather than in Brussels, and the new collective includes very different women, with different experiences and approaches. What we have in common is our disenchantment with reformism as a mode of relations and as a practice. I don't mean that we shouldn't take what we can get, but it feels as though all we ever do is fill in forms, fight over who gets what and so on. The GRIF doesn't want to get involved in all that. We also don't want to get involved in the business of putting out a feminist studies journal. Feminist studies seems to be replacing dialogue, and that is dangerous. Danielle spoke earlier of silencing, and of not having a way to be supportive but still to voice our criticisms of the government. Well that is what the GRIF wants to do – we must keep our critical perspective in what we do.

'Anglo-Saxon' feminism in France?

Rosi Braidotti: I can't fight for feminist studies: so they let us teach feminism, so what?
CD: What can you fight for?
Rosi Braidotti: Things that are important to our everyday existence, things that are close. For instance identity paper controls in the métro, or the very real poverty around us. The vast majority of the 'new poor' are women with children. You said that nobody here wanted to talk about racism or the peace movement, well there are good reasons for this – it's simply symptomatic of the lack of critical reflection in the movement. In the GRIF, we're at least doing something – in our next issue there will be something on unemployment.
CD: Do you think that you're going back to a more Anglo-Saxon approach?
Rosi Braidotti: Well, I'm going back to what I knew in my first feminist experiences in Australia, fighting for things around me – at least I know what I'm fighting for. Everything had become so abstract . . .

147

This maybe more 'Anglo-Saxon' approach seems on the whole to be the prerogative of the *Maison des femmes*, the women's centre in Paris. I had intended to go there, but illness prevented me from doing so. From what women told me, however, the *Maison des femmes* appears to be the centre of a more practical, probably more 'class struggle'-orientated feminism. The centre provides premises for many small collectives to meet, organises events and is not involved with the university-centred research-orientated feminist studies focus of many of the women I spoke to. While many women spoke regretfully of the lack of contact between different feminisms, nobody seemed really to want to try to bring women together, but seemed rather to accept the new situation. Only the *Maison des femmes* is planning a *rencontre*, a meeting, of this kind, like in 'the old days'.

An open letter to women dated 1 October 1984 called for this national meeting and set out the *Maison's* collective's feelings about the current state of the women's movement:

We haven't all got together for a long time now and there isn't much contact between us. For a while, some people have been proclaiming that feminism is dead, but we say that the women's movement is alive and well (. . .)

There are many women's, feminist, spaces in France – traditional women's associations or other types of association, especially outside Paris, where an enormous amount of work is being done for women in different ways – information on women's rights, vocational training, lesbian groups, shelters for battered women, short courses, workshops, research, publications, newsletters, centres, restaurants, businesses, co-ops . . .

Many of us at the centre think that the time is right for all these women to come together . . .

*   *   *

Overall, the women's movement may not be in a spectacular phase (is it in a spectacular phase anywhere?); it may not have the joy and excitement of the early days; the myth of sisterhood may no longer be operational; the movement, in growing up, may have slowed down and lost its youthful sense of community, but women are actively seeking new modes to replace the (already) old feminist models, and much is being done that is positive and productive:

Danielle Haase-Dubosc: Groups have tightened up I think – structures have been created where none existed before, have been made vertical where they had been horizontal. There are even majority and minority votes and executive committees . . . even women who are suspicious of structures are working in these groups and this is all very new. It seems to be working too – the three or four organisations that I belong to are certainly functional. And when I go to meetings, I feel that real work is being done, not that you waste three hours or so and then after most people leave, the decisions are made by the few women who stay behind.

I have the feeling that none of the women I knew in the movement have lost their commitment . . . we're in for a lifetime's struggle, probably beyond that, and we know it. We can't be satisfied with any results we may get, we have to keep pushing. I'm not pessimistic at all about things, and I think that a lot of the pessimism is simply learning to grow up. We thought we could change the world. (Rosi: I'm not a megalomaniac, but I really did think that we could change the world.) We have very few moments of uplift, but in terms of work and time, there is a great deal going on. We are working in different ways – I've been doing some things with UNESCO, with other more traditional women's associations, with our CNRS project . . . the feminism of the movement is all over the place now, it may not be a movement any more, but it's everywhere.

I was in a café the other evening and saw Edith Cresson, the Minister of Industry, being interviewed by a hard-hitting woman journalist on the 8 o'clock news. Cresson is the one to watch, she's doing a restructuring job on the image of women – doing a man's job – and the café was full of men watching, taking seriously an interview between two women. You wouldn't have seen this ten years ago. We shouldn't cry victory but we shouldn't ignore it either. In some ways we haven't made any progress at all but in others we have . . . things are changing and it's because of people like us that they are changing, I'm absolutely convinced of this . . . the glass isn't half empty, it's half full . . .

Notes

Chapter 1   Beginnings

1 Cited in Laure Adler, *Les Premières Journalistes* (Paris: Payot, 1979)p. 41.

2 Cited in Maité Albistur & Daniel Armogathe, *Histoire du féminisme français*, vol. 2 (Paris, éditions des femmes, 1977) pp. 428–9.

3 For the history of the feminism-socialism connection in the nineteenth century, see Charles Sowerwine, *Les Femmes et le socialisme* (FNSP, 1978) and Marilyn Jacoby Boxer's PhD thesis *Socialism Faces Feminism in France: 1879–1913* from University of California at Riverside, 1978. (Available from University Microfilms at Ann Arbor). For the current debates, see chapters 2, 6 and 7. Also, see *Féminisme et marxisme*, edited by the Communist *Elles Voient Rouge* collective (Tierce, 1981).

4 An anarchist cultural and artistic group.

5 Daniel Cohn-Bendit, *Obsolete Communism: The Leftwing Alternative* (Penguin, 1969) p.27.

6 In *Le Nouvel Observateur*, 20 May 1968.

7 In *Le Torchon brûle* (The Burning Rag) – the first feminist newspaper – No. 2., p.1, 1971.

8 *Libération des femmes: année zéro,* which first appeared as an issue of the journal *Partisans*, Nos. 54–55 in 1970, and was subsequently reprinted by Maspéro in 1972.

9 In *Le Torchon brûle*, No.0, p.3, 1970.

10. For the section that follows, I referred mainly to the feminist press of the 1970–1980 period (see the list at the beginning of the bibliography); also to Cathy Bernheim, *Perturbation ma soeur* (Seuil, 1983); Naty Garcia Guadilla, *Libération des femmes, le mlf* (PUF, 1981); Annie de Pisan and Ann Tristan, *Histoires du MLF* (Calmann-Lévy, 1977); *Douze Ans de femmes au quotidien*, by the *La Griffonne* collective (la Griffonne, 1981).

11 These examples are from Cathy Bernheim, *Perturbation ma soeur* in the chapter called *Le Temps de la colère*.

12 For a discussion of the Bobigny trial, see Chapter 3.

13 Françoise Picq, 'Sauve qui peut, le MLF' from *La Revue d'en face* No. 11, 1981 p.12. Translation forthcoming in *French Connections: Writings from the French Women's Movement* (Hutchinson, 1986), by Claire Duchen.

14 Of interest are the journals: *Le Torchon brûle, Les Pétroleuses, Femmes travailleuses en lutte, Elles voient rouge, Questions féministes, Mignonnes, allons voir sous la rose.*

15 In connection with this debate, see the work of feminist theorists Hélène Cixous and Luce Irigaray (discussed in Chapter 5); also the journals *Histoires d'elles, Les Cahiers du GRIF, des femmes en mouvements, Questions féministes, La Revue d'en face, Sorcières.*

16 Emmanuèle de Lesseps, 'Le Fait Féminin: et moi?' in *Questions féministes* No. 5, p.4, 1979.

17 Colette Guillaumin, 'Questions de différence' in *Questions féministes* No. 6, p.4, 1979. Translation forthcoming in *French Connections* (Hutchinson, 1986).

18 The title can't be directly translated. What is intended by the *en face* in the name, is the idea that the review is critical, at odds with established norms and politics. *en face* can also mean to face something squarely and directly as well as meaning that it is in opposition.

19 Catherine Ravelli, 'de l'intérêt de la féminitude pour le féminisme' in *La Revue d'en face*, No.4, p.25, 1978.

20 Nadja Ringart, 'La Naissance d'une secte' in *Libération*, 1 June 1977. Translation forthcoming in *French Connections* (Hutchinson, 1986).

21 Monique, in the dossier on heterosexuality and lesbianism in *La Revue d'en face*. No. 9/10, p.67, 1981. Translation in *Trouble and Strife* No.2, 1983.

Chapter 2   Currents: diversity and conflict

1 in *Les Pétroleuses*, No. 6, p.2, 1976.

2 Eliane Viennot, 'Féminisme et partis politiques: une greffe impossible?' in *Nouvelles Questions féministes* No. 2, 1981. Translation forthcoming.

3 For the full story of the *Psych et Po* attempted takeover, see *Chroniques d'une imposture* (Association pour les Luttes Féministes, 1981).

4 Dale Spender, *Man-Made Language* (Routledge & Kegan Paul, 1980) p.127.

5 Described in Barbara Sinclair Deckland, *The Women's Movement: Political, Socioeconomic and Psychological Issues* (Harper & Row, 1975) p.339.

6 Although the radical lesbians would not agree with a radical feminist claim to clarity . . .

Chapter 3   French feminists and motherhood: destiny or slavery?

1 In *Libération des femmes: Année Zéro*, op. cit., pp. 34–49.

2 Danièle Léger, in *Contraception et avortement* (CNRS, 1979) p.104. This is an excellent, perceptive analysis of the press coverage of the abortion and contraception issue.

3 The transcripts of the trial are published by the Association Choisir, *Avortement: une loi en procès, l'affaire de Bobigny* (Gallimard, 1973). The celebrities who testified included Simone de Beauvoir, Simone Iff (head of the French Family Planning Association, the MFPF), actresses Delphine Seyrig and Françoise Fabien, politician Michel Rocard, Nobel prize winner for medicine Jacques Monod and many other individuals: single mothers, midwives, and doctors.

4 Ibid., pp.189–190.

5 Gisèle Halimi, *La Cause des femmes* (Grasset, 1978) p.71.

6 In *le Livre Blanc de l'avortement* (Club de l'Observateur, 1971) p.28.

7 *Maternité esclave*, Les Chimères (UGE 10/18, 1975).

8 The debates leading up to the passing of the *loi Veil* can be read in *L'Avortement: histoire d'un débat*, edited by Bernard Pingaud (Flammarion, 1975).

9 In *Les Pétroleuses*, No. 1, 1974.

10 In a special issue of *Les Temps modernes*, April 1974, called *Les Femmes s'entêtent*, which was republished in 1975 (Gallimard). The title is a play on the surrealist *Femme 100 têtes/femmes sans tête*.

11 Ibid., p.2001.

12 *Jamais contentes*, No. 4–6, 1980.

Chapter 4   Feminists and (French) philosophy

1 The discussion in Jacques Derrida's work has a Western bias that is not addressed by feminists in their responses, concentrating as they do on woman-as-other. This bias can no doubt be defended by the fact that each culture has its own sameness/otherness.

2 Simone de Beauvoir, *Le Deuxième Sexe* vol. 1 (Gallimard, 1949) p.30.

3 Foucault's lectures began at 10 a.m. on Wednesday mornings. To be sure of a place, it was advisable to arrive before 9.30. He himself would arrive promptly at 10, with a few friends/students. The table at which he sat would be covered with cassette recorders, as was the floor surrounding the table. The only sound during the next hour, apart from Foucault's voice, would be the clicking of the cassette recorders as side A came to an end and the owners crept forward to change the tape . . .

4 Michel Foucault, in *Power/Knowledge* (Selected Interviews and other writings, 1972–1977) ed. Colin Gordon (Harvester Press, 1980) p.112.

5 Michel Foucault, *L'Archéologie du savoir* (Gallimard, 1969) translated by A.M. Sheridan Smith (Tavistock Publications, 1972) p.27.

6 Jonathan Culler, in *Structuralism and Since*, ed. John Sturrock (O.U.P., 1979) p.166.

7 *Différance* refers to the differentiation between language components and also to the act of deferment – the inevitable gap between the object of perception and our perception of it, passing as it does through language – that together create meaning.

153

8 Refusal of language, either altogether, or refusal to abide by its rules, in different forms of 'madness' could be interpreted as unconscious resistance. Even so, this kind of resistance still excludes the resistor from functioning in society.

9 Sherry Turkle, *Psychoanalytic Politics* (New York, Basic Books: 1978).

10 In *The Future of Difference,* edited by Hester Eisenstein and Alice Jardine (Boston, G.K. Hall and Barnard Women's Center: 1980) p.106.

11 I use 'his' advisedly. It is precisely the girl's entry into the Symbolic that has always been assumed to mirror the boy's, and that becomes the focus for feminist thinking about female psychosexual development.

12 For instance, feminists have examined the work of Plato, Marx, Rousseau and Freud (EG Luce Irigaray, *Speculum, de l'autre femme* (Minuit, 1974). Or for a very different approach, see Jean Bethke Elshstain, *Public Man, Private Woman* (Princeton U.P., 1981).

13 Lacan, from the seminar on feminine sexuality *Encore*, translated by Jacqueline Rose in *Feminine Sexuality* (Macmillan, 1982), edited by Jacqueline Rose & Juliet Mitchell, p.153.

14 Much fuss is always made about the untranslatability of *jouissance*. I understand *jouissance* in its usual sense of experience of sexual pleasure, and in its wider dictionary definition of taking pleasure in something, 'delighting in'.

Chapter 5   The concept of the feminine

1 Rosi Braidotti, *Féminisme et Philosophie*, Thèse de 3e cycle, University of Paris I, 1981, p.294.

2 This is from 'Sujet dans le langage et pratique politique' in ed. Verdiglione, *Psychanalyse et Politique* (Seuil, 1974) p.62 – as are the following quotations from Kristéva.

3 Luce Irigaray, *Ce Sexe qui n'en est pas un* (Minuit, 1977). Translation forthcoming with Cornell University Press.

4 Ibid., p.159.

5 French as a language does seem to lend itself to polysemantic practices, for instance, 'de' can mean 'from'/'of'/'some' and the context can deliberately leave the intended meaning ambiguous. Irigaray plays with

words extensively, adding a syllable, breaking up words, putting parts of words in parentheses. In this way she challenges (and the reader is forced to challenge) both meanings and the assumed transparency of language.

6 Luce Irigaray, op. cit., p.72.

7 Ibid., pp.62–3.

8 Ibid., p.132.

9 Ibid., p.138.

10 Ibid., p.77.

11 Ibid., p.27.

12 Ibid., p.205.

13 Ibid., p.209.

14 Hélène Cixous, 'Le Rire de la Méduse', *Arc 61*, 1975, p.39. Translated by Keith and Paula Cohen in *Signs*, Vol.I, No.4, 1976.

15 Héléne Cixous, *La Jeune Née*, eds. Cixous and Catherine Clément, (UGE, 1975) p.151.

16 Héléne Cixous, 'Le Sexe ou la tête' in *Les Cahiers du GRIF* No.13, 1976, p.14. Translated by Annette Kuhn in *Signs* Vol.7, No.1, Autumn 1981.

17 *La Jeune Née*, p.43.

18 Ibid., p.158.

19 'Le Sexe ou la tête', p.14.

20 *La Jeune Née*, p.171.

21 Ibid., p.45.

22 'Le Sexe ou la tête', Kuhn's translation, p.44.

23 *Psych et Po's* authoritarian undercurrents are quite in keeping with Lacan's highhanded attitude to his school and his followers.

24 *La Jeune Née*, p.119.

25 See Chapter 6.

Chapter 6   A different politics

1 For instance the Gaullist RPR (Rassemblement Pour la République) claims that 41 per cent of its members are women, but the percentage of women in the executive committee drops to 8 per cent. The PCF consistently has the greatest number of women at all levels of party hierarchy (but most of these women are not feminists . . .)

2 These investigations began after women were given the vote, to try to see the impact of the female vote. Most recently researchers Janine Mossuz-Lavau and Mariette Sineau at the *Centre d'Etudes sur la Vie Politique Française* have made women's voting patterns their own domain. See *Les Femmes et la politique* (PUF, 1983). Also see *Les femmes en France dans une société d'inégalités* (Documentation Française, 1982) a report commissioned by the Ministry for Women's Rights to examine women's situation in France in 1981.

3 These institutions, specific to France, show the belief that the State should train its own elites. Entry is through competitive examination, which theoretically guarantees equality of opportunity. Strangely enough, 90 per cent of the intake of ENA is composed of upper-middle class Parisian males, who are more equal than others.

4 There were women government Ministers in the 1936 Popular Front government at a time when women could neither vote nor stand for election. The French system which does not require a parliamentary past of its Ministers, allowed for this paradoxical situation.

5 See note 2 of this chapter.

6 Centre d'Etudes et de Recherches Marxistes (CERM), *La Condition féminine* (Editions Sociales, 1978) p.373.

7 This title plays on a sonnet by the poet Ronsard (*Les Amours*, XXIII):
Mignonne, levés-vous, vous estes paresseuse . . . .
Debout donque, allon voir l'herbelette perleuse
Et vostre beau rosier de boutons couronné . . . .

The rose is also the symbol of the socialist party, held in a fist. So, instead of being good girls as Ronsard would have it, feminists call for socialist women to examine the rose . . .

8 Huguette Bouchardeau, *Un coin dans leur monde* (Syros, 1981).

9 For the way that the socialist experiment has turned out, Chapter 7.

10 However, Bouchardeau herself has just (April 1985) resigned from the PSU to join the PS.

11 By Françoise Picq, 'Sauve qui peut le MLF', *op.cit.*

12 A reminder of the seven demands of the British women's liberation movement: 'The women's liberation movement asserts the right of every woman to a self-defined sexuality and demands:
   1 Equal pay
   2 Equal education and job opportunities
   3 Free contraception and abortion on demand
   4 Free 24-hour nurseries, under community control
   5 Legal and financial independence
   6 An end to discrimination against lesbians
   7 Freedom from intimidation by the threat or use of violence or sexual coercion, regardless of marital status. An end to the laws, assumptions and institutions that perpetuate male dominance and men's aggression towards women.'

Chapter 7 Feminism in Socialist France

1 The title of this chapter derives from the title of Françoise Ducrocq's article in *La Revue d'en Face* No.12, 1982; 'mouvement de libération des femmes en France socialiste' (the women's liberation movement in Socialist France).

2 The actual name of the Ministry was a disappointment to feminists: *de la femme* (of woman) uses a term that feminists reject as helping to perpetuate the myth that there is a thing called 'Woman' instead of many, different, individual women. My translation of the name (Ministry for Women's Rights) gives the Ministry the benefit of the doubt – it could properly be translated as the Ministry of the Rights of Woman.

3 This anti-sexist law came up against public (mostly male) outrage at the potential infringement of civil liberties, journalists cried 'censorship', feminists were accused of being puritans. The press coverage of the anti-sexist law debates can be found in *Les Temps Modernes*, July 1983, No.444. The law was later dropped.

4 Most women accept that the Ministry does useful work as far as it goes, but it simply does not go far enough.

5 In Rosi Braidotti's memorable expression, a 'femocracy'.

6 Thanks to Sian Reynolds for pointing out this contradiction.

7 Again, in Rosi Braidotti's words, the potential is there for a 'post-feminist solitude'.

8 Sometimes even this is not enough. This is why I like the term 'non-aligned' feminism, which is not synonymous with acceptance of any dogma.

9 Simone Iff, whom some women hoped would be the minister for Women's Rights, has been an adviser to Roudy, and is best known as the head of the French Family Planning Association. Huguette Bouchardeau is now Minister of the Environment.

10 Thanks to Ailbhe for a copy of her report. A shortened version appeared in the Women's Research and Resources Centre newsletter 1983, no.2.

Bibliography

Most of my 'sources' have been mentioned in footnotes. This bibliography
will serve as a pointer for readers who wish to follow up one aspect or
another of Feminism in France.

The feminist press

The feminist press may be consulted at the feminist library in Paris, the
Bibliothèque Marguerite Durand, 1 Place du Panthéon, 75005 Paris. Also
at the Bibliothèque Nationale, mostly at its Versailles branch, but some at
its Paris site in the Rue de Richelieu, 75001 Paris.
Le Torchon brûle (The Burning Rag); *Les Cahiers du féminisme* (The
Feminist Notebooks), magazine of the Ligue Communiste
Révolutionnaire women; *Les cahiers du Grif* (the GRIF notebooks) more
the theoretical in its orientation; *Colères!* (Anger/Angry) a 2 issue
anarchist women's newsletter/magazine; *des femmes en mouvements*,
both the *hebdo* and the *mensuelle*, and also *Le Quotidien des femmes*,
which were all *éditions des femmes* publications reflecting *Psych et Po*
preoccupations and language; *Elles voient rouge* (Women See Red) the
magazine of feminists in the PCF – now not in the PCF; *Femmes
travailleuses en lutte* (Women Workers' Struggle) a class struggle feminist
journal; *Histoires d'elles* (Her/Stories), a non-aligned magazine, which
tried to branch out to discuss many issues (violence, Iran, food . . .) and
not focus too intently on the MLF itself; *Jamais contentes* (Never Satisfied)
a non-aligned magazine, put out by younger women; *Mignonnes, allons
voir sous la rose* (impossible to translate) magazine of feminists in the PS –
now mostly not in the PS; *Nouvelles Féministes* (Feminist News) bulletin
of the League for Women's Rights, a 'reformist' group set up in 1974;
Questions féministes and *Nouvelles Questions féministes* (Feminist Issues

159

and New Feminist Issues), theoretical radical feminist journal; *Pénélope* (Penelope) magazine which is produced by a feminist group at the University of Paris VII and historians at the Centre de Recherches Historiques, and publishes reports of ongoing research, based each time around a theme; *les Pétroleuses* (the women incendiaries – so named after the claim that during the Paris Commune of 1871 women set fire to buildings in Paris, a claim never proven; women were still convicted of arson) – a class struggle publication; *La Revue d'en face*, (impossible to translate) a non-aligned magazine with consistently interesting and provocative articles; *Sorcières* (Sorceresses/Witches) a magazine focussing on women's relation to writing; *Le Temps des femmes* (Women's Time/Time for Women) a non-aligned newsletter. Many of these magazines and newsletters are no longer published. For the dates, see footnotes or mentions in the text.

History of Feminism/Feminist History

Maité Albistur and Daniel Armogathe (1977) *Histoire du féminisme français* (éditions des femmes); Huguette Bouchardeau (1977) *Pas d'histoire, les femmes* (Syros); Christiane Dufrancatel et al. (1979) *L'Histoire sans qualités* (Galilée); Annie de Pisan and Anne Tristan (1977) *Histoires de MLF* (Calmann-Lévy); Paule-Marie Duhet, *les femmes et la Révolution 1789–1794* (Julliard, 1971); Laure Adler, *Les Premières Journalistes* (Payot, 1979); *Mémoires de femmes, mémoire du peuple*, (Maspéro, 1979); Jean Rabaut, *Histoire des féminismes français* (Stock, 1978); Marie-Hélène Zylberberg-Hocquart, *Féminisme et syndicalisme en France* (Anthropos, 1978); see also the journal *Les Révoltes logiques*.
On the MLF, see especially, Cathy Bernheim *Perturbation ma soeur* (Seuil, 1983); Danièle Léger, *Le Féminisme en France* (Sycomore, 1982); and the feminist press.

Texts, Manifestoes and assorted books by feminists in France

Still essential reading – *Le Deuxième Sexe* by Simone de Beauvoir, (Gallimard 1949); Cercle Elisabeth Dmitriev, *Pour un féminisme autogestionnaire* (1975); les Chimères, *Maternité Esclave* (UGE, 1975); Choisir, *Avortement: une loi en procès, l'affaire de Bobigny* (1973) and *Le Programme Commun des Femmes* (1977); La Griffonne, *Douze ans de femmes au quotidien* (1981); *Libération des femmes: Année Zéro* (Maspéro, 1972); *Le Sexisme ordinaire* (Seuil, 1979)

French Philosophy and Feminist Theory

Roland Barthes, *Mythologies* (Seuil, 1957) and *Le Plaisir du texte* (Seuil, 1973); Jacques Derrida, *Positions* (1970) and *De la grammatologie* (1967) both published by the Editions de Minuit, *L'Ecriture et la différence* (Seuil, 1967). Good introductions to Derrida are in Gayatri Spivak's introduction to her translation of *Of Grammatology* and Barbara Johnson's introduction to her translation of *Disseminations;* Michel Foucault, *Les Mots et les choses* (Gallimard, 1966) and *L'Archéologie du savoir* (Gallimard, 1969); Jacques Lacan, *Ecrits* (2 vols, Seuil, 1966) and *Le Séminaire, livre XX, Encore* (Seuil, 1975). In English there are two books on French philosophy that are helpful: Vincent Descombes *Modern French Philosophy* (C.U.P., 1980) and *Structuralism and Since*, ed. by John Sturrock (O.U.P., 1979). Also on the connection between feminism and French psychoanalytic theory, see Jane Gallop, *Feminism and Psychoanalysis* (Macmillan, 1982). Feminist theory: as well as the women already mentioned or discussed in the text (mainly Cixous, Irigaray and Kristéva) see particularly Christine Delphy, whose collected articles are now available in English; *Close to Home* translated by Diana Leonard (Hutchinson, 1984). Also the work of Monique Plaza, Michèle Montrelay, Colette Guillaumin, Monique Wittig, Ann-Marie Dardigna, Evelyne le Garrec, Genevieve Fraisse, Rosi Braidotti, Françoise Collin, Michèle le Doeuff – to name only a few of the very many women doing interesting and varied work in fields from sociology to philosophy, to psychoanalysis and history. Most of their work is not yet translated. A few articles can be found in *Feminist Isssues*, which was published from California, but I personally found most of the translations unsatisfactory. Translation of Kristéva's work has been undertaken, and Cixous and Irigaray's work is currently being translated. Articles can be found in *Signs* and in *m/f* from time to time.

French political life

Many books have been published on May '68. I found most interesting: Daniel Cohn-Bendit, *Obsolete Communism. The Left-wing Alternative* (Penguin, 1969); *Les Murs ont la Parole* (Tchou, 1968); and Alfred Willener, *The Action-Image of Society* (Tavistock, 1970). See also Sherry Turkle, *Psychoanalytic Politics* (Basic Books, 1978), Neill Nugent and

David Lowe, *The Left in France* (Macmillan, 1982), Mark Poster,
Existential Marxism in Post-war France (Princeton U.P., 1975), Philip
Cerny (ed.) *Social Movements and Protest in France* (Frances Pinter 1982).
These books on the culture of protest are all very readable.
For a feminist view of political life, see Huguette Bouchardeau, *Un Coin
dans leur monde* (Syros, 1980); see the publication of the Ministry for
Women's Rights, *Citoyennes à part entière;* Odile Dhavernas, *Droits des
femmes, pouvoirs des hommes* (Seuil, 1978); and see the feminist press.
See also the works mentioned in footnotes.

Index

163

elections (1981), 39, 113, 115, 125
Elle conference, 9–10
Elles Voient Rouge, 19, 108; *see also*
    Parti Communiste Français

feminine, the, 34–6, 71, 79, 82–102;
    see also: difference; *Psychanalyse
    et Politique*; Cixous, Hélène;
    Irigaray, Luce; Kristéva, Julia
Féministes Révolutionnaires, 14, 16,
    17, 19, 40–1, 55–6, 69; *see also*
    non-aligned feminism
Femmes Travailleuses en Lutte, 28
Foucault, Michel, 68, 70, 72–3, 76,
    96, fn3. 153
Fouque, Antoinette, 21, 32, 35, 39,
    83, 137
Freeman, Jo, 45
French Revolution, 1
Fronde, la, 3

Gallop, Jane, 78
Giroud, Françoise, 127
groupe d'études féministes (GEF),
    143
groupe Information Santé (GIS), 53
Guillaumin, Colette, 141

Haase-Dubose, Danielle, 138, 149
Halimi, Gisèle, 15, 53, 54, 55; *see
    also Choisir*
Heterosexuality: as strategy of
    oppression, 22–5; as violence to
    women, 57; *see also* radical
    lesbianism
Histoires d'Elles, 20, 43, 142
Huston, Nancy, 142

Iff, Simone, 138
Irigaray, Luce, 71, 84, 87, 90, 95, 98,
    fn 155; *Ce Sexe Qui N'en Est Pas
    Un*, 88–9; *Quand Nos Lèvres Se
    Parlent*, 90–1; *Speculum, de
    l'autre femme*, 87–8

jouissance, 80, 89, 91, 96, 97, 98, 99,
    fn14.154

Kandel, Liliane, 37, 39, 136, 138, 140
Kristéva, Julia, 84, 85–7, 90, 99

Lacan, Jacques, 34, 69, 70, 73, 77–81,
    84–97, 100
Léger, Danièle, 52
lesbian movement, 137
Libérer nos corps . . ., 55–6
libidinal economy, 34, 81, 91–2,
    95–6, 98, 101
Logos, 35, 74, 84, 92
loi Neuwirth, 4

maison des femmes, 148
Manifesto of the 343, 12, 52, 53, 111
Marxism, 30, 69, 71; *see also Parti
    Communiste Français*
masculinity, 20, 63, 79, 91, 93, 99; *see
    also* phallogocentrism
Maternité Esclave, 55–6
May '68, events of, 1, 5–9, 68, 77;
    influence on MLF, 8; women in,
    7–8
Ministry for Women's Rights, 39,
    105, 127–31, 135, 139, 145
Mignonnes, allons voir sous la rose,
    113, 116; *see also courant G*; *Parti
    Socialiste*
misogyny, 35, 71, 84
Mitterrand, François, 4, 113, 115,
    125, 139
motherhood, 49–66; childbirth, 62–
    3; class struggle current on, 51–2,
    56–7; non-aligned feminists on,
    61–6; pregnancy, 61–2;
    Psychanalyse et Politique on, 59,
    63; woman-as-mother, 64–6
*Mouvement de Liberation des
    Femmes* (MLF): birth of, 4–16, *see
    also* May '68; currents in, 17–18,
    27–47, *see also* class struggle
    current, *Féministes
    Révolutionnaires*, non-aligned
    feminism, *Psychanalyse et
    Politique*; relation to political
    parties, 27, 29–30, 103–20;
    relation to Socialist Government,
    125–49; since 1981, 125–49;